IELTS対策シリーズ

改訂新装版　International English Language Testing System

IELTS
ライティング
完全対策

嶋津幸樹 著
Koki Shimazu

アルク

はじめに

5.5 → 7.0 の道のり

　私の英語学習の旅における一番の障壁は、IELTSのライティングでした。そして、IELTSの日本人受験者の平均スコアが最も低いセクションも、ライティングです。この英語学習者の誰もが超えなければならない高い壁を、どのようにしたら効率よく限られた時間の中で超えられるのか？ 大学院受験のときに半年間、IELTSのライティング対策のみを繰り返し、その答えが見つかりました。

　大学3年時、初めてIELTSを受験して**世界基準の英語**に出会った感覚を今でも覚えています。そのときの気持ちを一言で表すと、**自信喪失**です。特にライティングに関しては、それまで1時間という制限時間内に計400語ものエッセーを書いた経験などなく、与えられた題材に関して考えたことも議論をしたこともありませんでした。ありとあらゆる対策をして既存の

問題集を読破し、四六時中IELTSのことばかり考えていました。しかし、自分なりの対策を繰り返し何度挑戦しても、バンドスコア7.0の壁が超えられませんでした。

もがき苦しむも、なかなかスコアが上がらない日々

　単語帳をボロボロになるまで繰り返し使い、文法書を読み漁_{あさ}り、我武者羅_{がむしゃら}にエッセーを書き、あらゆる対策をしても、7.0の壁は高く超えられずに悩んでいました。しかしライティング対策を始めて半年後、元IELTS試験官の方にエッセーを添削していただく機会があり、**ある2つの鉄則**に気がつきました。

　それは、エッセーで使える汎用性のあるライティングの<u>型</u>と、多彩な表現に言い換える**パラフレーズ**の力です。「型」とは、ランダムに創り上げたものではなく実際にネイティブが使う「型」です。そのとき私の文章について指摘されたのは、まず「通じるけど違和感がある」「文法的に間違っていないけど使わない」といった、ネイティブ感覚の欠如でした。そしてもう1つは、表現が豊富でないことでした。単調な表現や高頻出語彙のみで構成された文章では、高得点は狙えません。この2つを意識し始めてから、私の英語学習の旅は明るくなりました。

鉄則に気づき、道がひらけた

　その後の受験でライティングのバンドスコアが7.0を超え、最終的に7.5を獲得することができました。同時に他のスキルも向上し、**オーバーオールで8.0を超え**、大学院でのエッセーの課題も難なくこなすことができるようになりました。そして、その後も継続した英語学習を通して、アカデミックライティングの奥深さと、洗練されたエッセーの美しさを感じるようになっていきました。

　この本を通して、皆さんにもそれを体感していただきたいと願っています。まずは3カ月この本を使い込んでください。ライティングで合格点を取る力がつくのはもちろん、世界基準の英語に出会えます！

嶋津幸樹

改訂新装版 IELTSライティング完全対策

Contents

本書の特長

実践重視型の構成

　IELTSで求められるライティング技能を無理なく確実に身につける
ため、まずは頻出テーマごとに短文を書く練習で基礎を固めます。そ
の後、本番さながらの模擬問題20問に取り組みます。

　各問題には、エッセーの構想の仕方が分かるBrainstormingのコー
ナーがあり、解答例のモデルエッセーと対照できます。解説ページで
は、エッセーのパラグラフ単位で書き方を学ぶことができます。

本番の頻出テーマをすべてカバー

　IELTSの本試験と同等のクオリティの模擬問題を用意しています。

　20問で頻出テーマを網羅しており、これらに取り組むことで万全な
ライティング対策ができます。

見開きごとに問題再掲。学びやすいレイアウト

　模擬問題の解説ページは、「導入（Introduction）」「本論1（Body 1）」
「本論2（Body 2）」「結論（Conclusion）」のパラグラフごとに1見開
きになっており、学びやすくレイアウトされています。

　それぞれの見開きに問題が再掲載されているため、最初のページに
戻って問題を確認する手間が省けます。

※「結論」がないエッセーや、「本論3」があるエッセーもあります。

確実に7.0を取るための「型」が習得できる

　本書の主目的は、5.5 ～ 6.5レベルの日本人学習者が7.0の壁を効率
的に超えることです。学習者が自分の現在の力よりやや高いレベルの
文章から自分の「型」を見つけ、目標を達成できるようになっています。

学習の進め方

1問解くたび実力アップ！

本書の学習ページは、短文を書く練習をする第2章（Warming Up）と、IELTSのライティングテストの模擬問題20問に挑戦する第3章・第4章から成っています。いずれも、2ページの見開き単位で学習が進められます。

Warming Up（第2章）

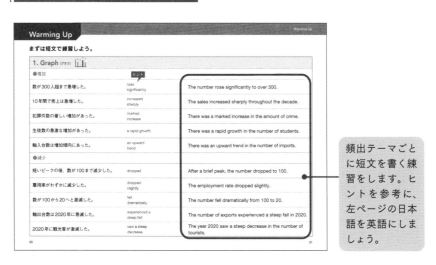

頻出テーマごとに短文を書く練習をします。ヒントを参考に、左ページの日本語を英語にしましょう。

20の模擬問題（第3章、第4章）

▶ 問題・Brainstorming・モデルエッセー

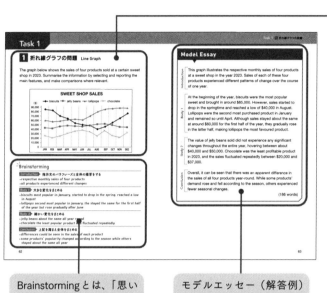

問題が掲載されています。問われていることに確実に答えるエッセーを書くために、注意深く読みましょう。

Brainstormingとは、「思いつくままにアイデアを出すこと」です。エッセーの構想の練り方や、書く前の下準備の参考にしてください。

モデルエッセー（解答例）の全文です。Brainstormingと照らし合わせると、流れや構成の作り方がより明確になります。

▶ 解説（パラグラフごとに見開きで掲載）

導入（Introduction）

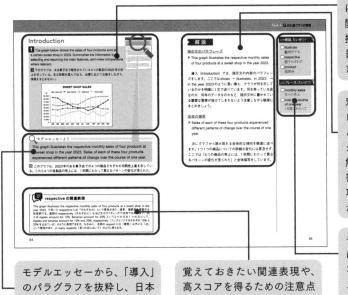

解説ページでは、すべての見開きに問題が再掲載され、その日本語訳があります。

着眼点やパラフレーズの方法など、ライティングのポイントを解説しています。書く際の重要事項を具体的につかみましょう。

モデルエッセーに出てきた重要な単語とフレーズをチェックできます。

モデルエッセーから、「導入」のパラグラフを抜粋し、日本語訳とともに掲載しています。

覚えておきたい関連表現や、高スコアを得るための注意点など、お役立ち情報満載のコラムを多数用意しています。

本論1（Body 1）　※本論2または本論3まで同様

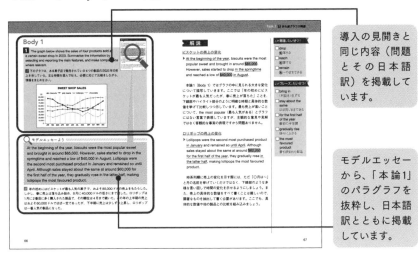

導入の見開きと同じ内容（問題とその日本語訳）を掲載しています。

モデルエッセーから、「本論1」のパラグラフを抜粋し、日本語訳とともに掲載しています。

結論 (Conclusion)

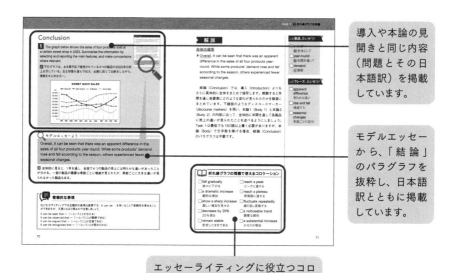

導入や本論の見開きと同じ内容（問題とその日本語訳）を掲載しています。

モデルエッセーから、「結論」のパラグラフを抜粋し、日本語訳とともに掲載しています。

エッセーライティングに役立つコロケーション（相性の良い単語同士の結びつき）の例を紹介しています。

第 1 章

Introduction

IELTS とは

　International English Language Testing System（IELTS：アイエルツ）は、イギリスやオーストラリアなどへの留学や英語圏移住を目的とした方の英語力を証明するための英語のテストです。近年では日本人受験者も急増し、世界で最も正確に英語力を測る4技能のテストの1つとして知られています。

Academic Module
（アカデミック・モジュール）

　大学や大学院に入学するのに必要な英語力があるかを見極めるテスト。本書はこちらの対策用書籍です。

General Training Module
（ジェネラル・トレーニング・モジュール）

　仕事や研修、移住申請を目的とした受験者向けのテストです。

● IELTS の構成と採点

　IELTS は英語の4技能であるライティング、リーディング、リスニング、スピーキングの4つのテストで構成されています。テストの成績は、上記それぞれについて1.0～9.0の0.5刻みのバンドスコアで示され、また4技能をまとめた総合評価としてのオーバーオール・バンドスコアが、同様に1.0～9.0で示されます。

　一般的に、英語圏の大学に進学するにあたって必要とされるスコアは6.0です。世界ランキング100位以内に入る大学では、学部によって異なりますが、6.5が必要な場合もあり、オックスフォード大学やケンブリッジ大学では7.0が必要となります。

9	エキスパート ユーザー	十分に英語を駆使する能力を有している。適切、正確かつ流暢で、完全な理解力もある。
8	非常に優秀な ユーザー	時折、非体系的な不正確さや不適切さが見られるものの、十分に英語を駆使する能力を有している。慣れない状況においては、誤解が生ずる可能性もある。込み入った議論にも対応できる。
7	優秀な ユーザー	時折、不正確さや不適切さが見られ、また状況によっては誤解が生ずる可能性もあるが、英語を駆使する能力を有している。複雑な言語にも概して対応でき、詳細な論理を理解できる。
6	有能な ユーザー	不正確さ、不適切さ、および誤解がいくらか見られるものの、概して効果的に英語を駆使する能力を有している。特に、慣れた状況においては、かなり複雑な言語の使用と理解ができる。
5	中程度の ユーザー	部分的に英語を駆使する能力を有しており、ほとんどの状況において大まかな意味をつかむことができる。ただし、多くの間違いを犯すことも予想される。自身の専門分野では、基本的なコミュニケーションを行うことができる。
4	限定的な ユーザー	慣れた状況においてのみ、基本的能力を発揮できる。理解力、表現力の問題が頻繁に見られる。複雑な言語は使用できない。
3	非常に限定的な ユーザー	非常に慣れた状況において、一般的な意味のみを伝え、理解することができる。コミュニケーションが頻繁に途絶える。
2	散発的な ユーザー	慣れた状況下で、その場の必要性に対処するため、極めて基本的な情報を単語の羅列や短い定型句を用いて伝える以外に、現実的なコミュニケーションを行うことは不可能。英語による会話や文章を理解するのに非常に苦労する。
1	非ユーザー	いくつかの単語を羅列して用いることしかできず、基本的に英語を使用する能力を有していない。
0	試験放棄	評価可能な情報なし。

（参考　https://ieltsjp.com/japan/about/about-ielts/ielts-band-scores）

IELTSライティングテストの概要

ライティングテストの内容

問題数	2問
試験時間	60分
内容	〈Task 1〉　回答時間の目安：20分 グラフ、表などの情報を整理し、150語以上で描写する。 〈Task 2〉　回答時間の目安：40分 テーマが与えられ、250語以上で自分の意見を述べる。

ライティングテストの採点基準

Task 1　150語以上	Task 2　250語以上
◆ 課題の達成度	◆ 課題への回答
◆ 一貫性とまとまり	◆ 一貫性とまとまり
◆ 語彙力	◆ 語彙力
◆ 文法知識と正確さ	◆ 文法知識と正確さ

評価基準の詳細は以下の通りです。

Task 1のみ
◆ 課題の達成度 （Task Achievement）
- 情報における重要で顕著な特徴を厳選する
- 提示された特徴の詳細を正確に明示する
- グラフや表に示された数字を描写する
- 主要な変化や特徴を客観的に比較・対照する

Task 2のみ

◆ 課題への回答 （Task Response）

- 指示文のタスクを明確に読み取る
- 導入と結論で、指示文に回答していることを正確に明示する
- 「議論・意見型」「賛成・反対型」「課題解決型」のどのタスクかを把握する
- タスクに関連した主題文と、それに伴う支持文を客観的に展開する

Task 1、Task 2共通

◆ 一貫性とまとまり （Coherence and Cohesion）

- 情報の特徴を順序立てて構成する
- 情報や議論を論理的に展開し構成する
- 指示文を適切にパラフレーズする
- 各パラグラフで、適切なディスコースマーカー（接続表現）を適切な場所で使用する

◆ 語彙力 （Lexical Resource）

- 基本語を正確に用いて表現する
- 繰り返しやスペリングの誤りを避ける
- テーマにふさわしい定型表現を用いる
- 難易度の高い語彙とフレーズで表現する

◆ 文法知識と正確さ （Grammatical Range and Accuracy）

- 基本文法を正確に使用する
- 単文だけでなく、重文や複文も用いて表現する
- コンマやピリオド、ハイフンなどの記号を正確に使用する
- 受動態や分詞構文など、複雑な文法を使用する

Task 1の書き方

　Task 1は基本的に、導入（**Introduction**）、本論1（**Body 1**）、本論2（**Body 2**）、結論（**Conclusion**）の4パラグラフから成るエッセーで、グラフやチャート、地図やプロセスなどを描写します。1つのグラフを描写するシンプルなものから、2つの地図の変化や違いを比較するもの、物質や製品が出来上がるまでのプロセスを描写するものまで、幅広く出題されます。語数は150語以上です。

　導入（Introduction）では、①指示文のパラフレーズ（**Paraphrasing**）と②全体の描写（**Overall Description**）を行います。①では、下の例のように指示文を自分なりの表現を使って言い換えます。②では、グラフなどから読み取れる重要な要素を簡潔にまとめます。

　　例 The bar graph shows ... → The data in the bar graph displays ...
　　例 sales for a year → annual sales

　本論1（Body 1）と本論2（Body 2）では、パラグラフごとにより細かい描写を行います。本論1（Body 1）で大きな違いをまとめた場合は、本論2（Body 2）で小さな違いをまとめます。グラフなどからまんべんなく情報を拾い、分析・比較・要約しながら全体を均等に描写することが大切です。

　結論（Conclusion）では再び全体の描写（**Overall Description**）を行います。基本的には本論1（Body 1）と本論2（Body 2）の内容を簡潔にまとめ、導入（Introduction）の全体の描写よりも具体的になるようにします。その際、個人的な感想や評価は厳禁です。客観的な描写を心がけましょう。なお、Task 1では結論（Conclusion）は必須ではありませんが、本論（Body）の内容をあらためてまとめる必要があるときや、語数を稼ぎたいときに追加します。

各パラグラフの内容

導入（Introduction）

①指示文のパラフレーズ（Paraphrasing）
②全体の描写（Overall Description）

本論 1（Body 1）

大きな違いをまとめる

本論 2（Body 2）

小さな違いをまとめる

結論（Conclusion）

全体の描写（Overall Description）

Task 2の書き方

　テーマについての自分の意見を250語以上で書くTask 2では、アカデミックライティングのスキルがより求められます。Task 1のエッセーと同様に、導入（**Introduction**）、本論（**Body**）、結論（**Conclusion**）の流れで議論を展開していきます。主観的な感想文ではなく、誰もがうなずける論理的・客観的な内容である必要があります。

　導入（Introduction）では、読み手になじみのある背景情報を組み込んだ①一般文（**General Statement**）を書きます。ここでは一般的な事実や最近の動向などを、客観的に描写します。次に②エッセー全体の主題文（**Thesis Statement**）では、自分の意見や立場とトピックの要点を、指示文をパラフレーズしながら簡潔にまとめます。このパラグラフを読むだけでエッセーの概要が読み取れるようにしましょう。

　本論1（Body 1）と本論2（Body 2）は同じ構成で、①パラグラフの主題文（**Topic Sentence**）と②支持文（**Supporting Sentence**）から成り立っています。①パラグラフの主題文は、そのパラグラフの内容が簡潔に集約されている重要な文です。この文で自分の主張と一般論を展開し、②支持文で主張を裏づける根拠を述べて①での見解を強固にしていきます。支持文は複数あることも多く、However（しかしながら）やIn addition（さらに）などの接続表現（**ディスコースマーカー：discourse markers**）を使い、一貫性のある議論を展開していきます。

　結論（Conclusion）の①要約文（**Summarising Sentence**）で、エッセーの要点を簡潔に述べます。その際、導入（Introduction）の②エッセー全体の主題文（**Thesis Statement**）と同様の内容を組み込みます。そして最後に、③結論文（**Concluding Sentence**）で未来の展望などを述べ、エッセーを結論づけます。

各パラグラフの内容

導入 (Introduction)

①一般文 (General Statement)
②エッセー全体の主題文 (Thesis Statement)

本論 1 (Body 1)

①パラグラフの主題文 (Topic Sentence)
②支持文 (Supporting Sentence)

本論 2 (Body 2)

①パラグラフの主題文 (Topic Sentence)
②支持文 (Supporting Sentence)

結論 (Conclusion)

①要約文 (Summarising Sentence)
②結論文 (Concluding Sentence)

ライティングで高得点を取るための
5つの力
ちから

① 語彙力（Vocabulary）

　ライティングにおいては、読んだり聞いたりして分かる受動語彙（receptive vocabulary）だけでなく、書いたり話したりするための発表語彙（productive vocabulary）が必要となります。受動語彙についてはビジュアルや語源の知識を活用しながら効率的に大量のインプットを行い、発表語彙については基本語を正確に身につけ適切に使用できるようにしていきましょう！

② 表現力

　自分の語彙や表現のレパートリーに磨きをかけ、さまざまな状況に合った豊富な表現を引き出す練習をしていきましょう！
　美しいエッセーにたくさん触れることで、質の高い英文や表現をインプットできます。ライティング向上の一番の近道は、美しいエッセーの大量のインプットです。その作業を繰り返しながら、1つの事柄を多角的な視点から描写する習慣をつけ、多彩な表現を引き出せるようにすることが重要です。語彙や表現を使える形で身につけ、誰も

がうなるような美しいエッセーで自分を表現できるようにしていきましょう。

③ 情報力

　IELTSのライティングでは、日常的な話題から、英語のニュースに登場するようなグラフや社会問題まで、幅広いテーマが扱われます。それらのテーマを常日頃から意識し、批判的に思考し、自分なりの意見を確立しておくことが大切です。主観的な考えや経験だけでなく、客観的な証拠やデータを集め、自分の意見を説得力のあるものにする訓練も必要です。日々の学習で知識教養を身につけ、時事問題に触れ、情報力を養いましょう。

④ 応用力

　美しいエッセーには、まねしたくなる「型」が存在します。その「型」の応用スキルが、IELTSのライティングにおける高得点獲得のカギです。本書に掲載しているエッセーは、まねしたくなるような美しい「型」の宝庫です。美しいエッセーを書く癖をつけると、そこで使われている表現を別の場面でも使えるようになります。どのようなトピックにも応用できる「型」を英語の記事や学術論文からインプットし、汎用性のある自分独自の「型」にしていきましょう！

⑤ 忍耐力

　筋トレをしてもすぐには筋肉がつかないように、英語学習も短期間で成果を出すことは至難の業です。特にライティングは成果が見えにくく、学習のモチベーションを保つのが難しい分野でもあります。3カ月間、毎日英文を書くトレーニングを繰り返すと、ようやく自分なりの「型」が確立されてきます。着実に読み、着実に新たな表現に触れ、着実にアウトプットを繰り返すことが、本質的な英語力を身につけIELTSのライティングで高得点を獲得するための近道です。

2つの鉄則を徹底的にたたき込む

1. 汎用性のあるアカデミックライティングの「型」

　アカデミックライティングの「型」を、構文やコロケーションなど定型表現と呼ばれる英語表現の「型」も含めて身につけることが、IELTSにおけるライティング攻略のカギです。ここでは、本書で扱っている5つの重要な要素を簡単に紹介します。

① 客観性（Objectivity）

　アカデミックライティングや学術論文において最も重要なことは、主観的な（subjective）感想や根拠なしの主張ではなく、客観的な（objective）事実や法則を記述し、論理的な（logical）文章を書くことです。IELTSのライティングTask 1は図やデータを描写するタスクですが、主観的な意見や記載のない情報を盛り込むことは厳禁です。Task 2は誰もがうなずける一般文（General Statement）から始め、読み手が納得できる結論文（Concluding Sentence）を導き出すことが重要です。

② 構成（Organisation）

　アカデミックライティングの基本構成は、導入（Introduction）、本論（Body）、結論（Conclusion）です。論理的な展開をするために、パラグラフごとにルールがあります。IELTSの評価基準には「一貫性とまとまり（Coherence and Cohesion）」があるため、話の展開の方向性を示唆する接続詞・副詞・前置詞といった接続表現であるディスコースマーカー（discourse markers）を用いて、一貫性が保たれ構成のしっかりした英文を、Task 1では150語以上、Task 2では250語以上で書く必要があります。

③ 主張（Argument）

　アカデミックライティングでは客観的な主張が求められます。支持文（Supporting Sentences）では、主張の根拠を成す4つのEと呼ばれるexample（具体例）、explanation（説明）、experience（経験）、evidence（証拠）を意識して、自分の主張を補強していきましょう。そして主張を和らげるヘッジング（hedging）の表現や法助動詞、また譲歩などを用いて、断定的になるのを避けるようにしましょう。Task 2の導入（Introduction）と結論（Conclusion）における主張の書き方がスコアを左右します。

④ シンプルであること（Simplicity）

　アカデミックライティングの神髄は、シンプルであることです。美しさが求められる世界には、Less is more.（少ないほうが良い）やKeep it simple.（シンプルにせよ）といった言葉が存在します。またシェイクスピアの代表作『ハムレット』にもBrevity is the soul of wit.（簡潔は分別の魂）という表現が出てきます。シンプルさ（simplicity）、簡潔さ（conciseness）、正確さ（precision）、この3つの要素が評価基準の1つ「文法知識と正確さ（Grammatical Range and Accuracy）」につながります。くどい表現や繰り返しを避け、シンプルであることを目指しましょう。

⑤ 言語使用領域（Register）

　アカデミックライティングでは、口語表現（colloquial expression）やスラング（slang）、決まり文句（cliché）やことわざ（proverb）、婉曲表現（euphemism）の使用は厳禁です。また、誇張や感情的な言葉も好まれません。フォーマル度を高め、性差別表現を避け、特定のグループに不快感を与えないポリティカル・コレクトネス（political correctness）を意識した、適切な言葉選びを心がけましょう。

2. 多彩な表現への言い換え：パラフレーズ

　パラフレーズ（paraphrasing）とは、原文の主張を保ちながら他の言葉で言い換えることです。IELTSのライティングで高得点を狙うには、パラフレーズの技術が不可欠です。ここでは、本書で扱っている、パラフレーズを実践する上で重要な5つの要素を簡単に紹介します。

① 語彙（Lexis）

　IELTSのライティングでは、基本語彙（basic vocabulary）を正確な語法で適切に用いることと、テーマ別の低頻出語彙（low frequency vocabulary）の正確な使用が高得点につながります。句動詞（phrasal verb）などの、会話で用いられる口語表現ではなく、アカデミックワードリスト（AWL：Academic Word List）に掲載されるような学術的語彙の使用を心がけてパラフレーズしましょう。

② 語源（Etymology）

　すべての英単語や英語表現にはストーリーがあります。歴史をひもとき、語源解釈を通して英単語を学習すると、語彙を効率的に増強できます。1066年のノルマン・コンクエスト（The Norman Conquest）から始まった、庶民が英語を話し、貴族がフランス語を用いる時代に、英語にはフランス語から借用した言葉が多数入り込みました。そのような単語の由来や、意味を持つ最小の言語単位である形態素と接頭辞・接尾辞に関する知識を活用して、高度な表現に言い換える力を磨きましょう。

③　類義語（Synonyms）

　パラフレーズの基本は、類義語に言い換えることです。Task 1 の指示文に頻出の show は、よりフォーマルな represent に言い換えることができ、Task 2 では、good をより洗練された beneficial などに言い換えることができます。高度な表現に言い換えることにより、同じ語の繰り返しを避けることができ、文章が豊かになります。高度な表現を使用するときには、同語反復や冗長さを避ける注意も必要です。日頃から英英辞典や類語辞典を活用して、表現の幅を広げましょう。

④　名詞化（Nominalisation）

　文法構造を変えることでパラフレーズすることもできます。その代表例に名詞化があります。動詞や形容詞を名詞にすることで、受動態や無生物主語の文を作ることができます。例えば、Because the scholarship was available, I was able to go abroad. （奨学金が利用できたので、海外に行くことができた）という文は、The availability of the scholarship made it possible to go abroad. に言い換えることで、より客観性のあるものになります。

⑤　翻訳（Translation）

　本書を手に取られた方の多くは、第一言語（L1）が英語ではないと思われますが、そのことは英語を学ぶ上で貴重な財産になります。英語のみで思考するのではなく、表現したい内容を日本語に翻訳してからパラフレーズする表現を考えるようにすると、表現の幅を広げやすくなります。その際、定型表現である英語のコロケーション（collocation）を豊富にインプットしておくことで、自然な表現が自然な文脈で出てくるようになります。

IELTS Writing

第2章

Warming Up

Task 1

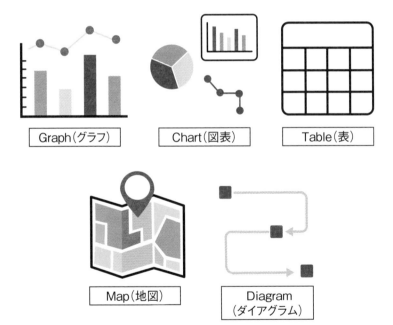

Graph（グラフ）　Chart（図表）　Table（表）

Map（地図）　Diagram（ダイアグラム）

まずは短文で練習しよう。

1. Graph (グラフ)

●増加

ヒント

日本語	ヒント
数が300人超まで急増した。	rose significantly
10年間で売上は急増した。	increased sharply
犯罪件数の著しい増加があった。	marked increase
生徒数の急激な増加があった。	a rapid growth
輸入台数は増加傾向にあった。	an upward trend

●減少

日本語	ヒント
短いピークの後、数が100まで減少した。	dropped
雇用率がわずかに減少した。	dropped slightly
数が100から20へと激減した。	fell dramatically
輸出台数は2020年に急減した。	experienced a steep fall
2020年に観光客が激減した。	saw a steep decrease

The number rose significantly to over 300.

The sales increased sharply throughout the decade.

There was a marked increase in the amount of crime.

There was a rapid growth in the number of students.

There was an upward trend in the number of imports.

After a brief peak, the number dropped to 100.

The employment rate dropped slightly.

The number fell dramatically from 100 to 20.

The number of exports experienced a steep fall in 2020.

The year 2020 saw a steep decrease in the number of tourists.

●変動	ヒント
その期間を通して数が低いままであった。	remained
その数は毎年変動している。	fluctuates
売上数が2000年にピークを迎えた。	peaked
その割合は30年間一定であった。	remained constant
自動車の数にわずかな変動があった。	minor fluctuations
●安定	
チケット売上は初年度、安定的に推移した。	remained stable
イルカの数は安定していた。	remained steady
自動車の売上は4年間横ばいであった。	stayed unchanged
苦情はわずか2カ月で頭打ちになった。	reached a plateau
この期間に犯罪率は横ばいとなった。	levelled off

The number remained low over the period.

The number fluctuates each year.

The number of sales peaked in 2000.

The percentage remained constant over three decades.

There were minor fluctuations in the number of cars.

Ticket sales remained stable in the first year.

Dolphin numbers remained steady.

Car sales stayed unchanged for four years.

Complaints reached a plateau in just two months.

Crime rates levelled off in this period.

2. Chart (図表)

卒業生がその表の30%を占める。	account for
自転車が円グラフのほぼ半分を占めている。	makes up
海外からの利益は収益の約半分を占めている。	constitute
生産量がほぼ2倍になった。	nearly doubled
小説の数は漫画の数のほぼ3分の1である。	nearly a third
その会社は2000年に大きな変化があった。	experienced
観光客数は大きく減少した。	witnessed
2つの円グラフは性別間での色の選択を比較している。	compare
その図は車両の使用に関するデータを示している。	provides
その図から消費量が減少したことが明らかである。	evident

Graduates account for 30% of the chart.

Bicycle makes up almost half of the pie chart.

Profits from overseas constitute about a half of revenue.

The amount of production nearly doubled.

The number of novels is nearly a third of that of comic books.

The company experienced major changes in the year 2000.

The number of tourists witnessed a significant drop.

The two pie charts compare the colour choices between genders.

The chart provides data about the use of vehicles.

It is evident from the chart that the consumption decreased.

3. Table (表)

日本語	ヒント
サッカーは野球と同じくらい人気がある。	as popular as
クリケットはサッカーほど人気がない。	not as popular as
空手の人気は柔道よりも高い。	higher than
スポーツは見るよりやるほうがいい。	better than
最も割合が高かったのはスキーだった。	The largest
ラグビーが最も人気のスポーツだった。	the most
卓球がすべての中で最も人気がなかった。	the least
バドミントンが最も低い数字だった。	the lowest
ゴルフが2番目に人気のスポーツだった。	second most popular
サッカーが圧倒的に人気のスポーツだった。	by far the most popular

Football is as popular as baseball.

Cricket is not as popular as football.

The popularity of karate is higher than that of judo.

Playing sports is better than watching sports.

The largest proportion was skiing.

Rugby was the most popular sport.

Table tennis was the least popular of all.

Badminton had the lowest figures.

Golf was the second most popular sport.

Football was by far the most popular sport.

4. Map (地図)

	ヒント
その部屋は南向きである。	faces
ホテルはバス停の向かいにある。	is across from
博物館は図書館の横に位置している。	is located next to
新しい博物館がその場所に建設予定である。	is set to be
地図上の太い線が道路に相当する。	correspond to
その駐車場は拡大された。	was enlarged
その家々は取り壊された。	were demolished
その駅は博物館になった。	was made into
その空港は北に移設された。	was relocated
エントランスホールは近代化された。	was modernised

The room faces south.

The hotel is across from the bus stop.

The museum is located next to the library.

A new museum is set to be built in its place.

The broad lines on the map correspond to roads.

The parking area was enlarged.

The houses were demolished.

The station was made into a museum.

The airport was relocated to the north.

The entrance hall was modernised.

5. Diagram (ダイアグラム)

自動車の製造には6つの段階がある。	steps
この製作工程は合計で5日間かかる。	process
その過程には5つの段階がある。	in the process
最初のステージでは、製品が店に配達される。	In the first stage
最後の段階では、製品を梱包する。	The last step
この時点で、製品は検査される。	At this point
加工が終わると、それは検査場に運ばれる。	Once it is
最終ステージで、それは密封されラベルを貼られる。	In the final stage
続いて、それは各店舗に配送される。	Subsequently
これに続いて、その装置は次のステージに移される。	Following this

There are six steps in the production of cars.

This production process takes five days in total.

There are five steps in the process.

In the first stage, products are delivered to the store.

The last step is to pack the product.

At this point, the product is inspected.

Once it is processed, it is taken to the inspection area.

In the final stage, it is sealed and labelled.

Subsequently, it is distributed to the respective stores.

Following this, the device is transferred to the next stage.

Memo

Task 2

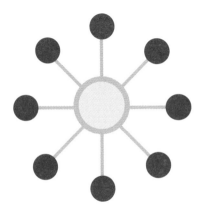

1. General（一般）
2. Nature（自然）
3. Education（教育）
4. Science（科学）
5. Society（社会）
6. Transport（交通）
7. Health（健康）
8. Economy（経済）

Warming Up

まずは短文で練習しよう。

1. General （一般）

ヒント

日本は人気である。	is
塩は重要であった。	was
オーロラは美しい。	are
日本人は礼儀正しい。	are
私の両親は協力的であった。	were
教師は残業をする。	work
子どもは警察官に憧れる。	admire
赤は太陽を表している。	represents
日本の人口が減った。	diminished
神が世界を創造した。	created

Japan is popular.

Salt was important.

Auroras are beautiful.

Japanese people are polite.

My parents were supportive.

Teachers work overtime.

Children admire police officers.

The red represents the sun.

The population diminished in Japan.

God created the world.

2. Nature (自然)

鳥は飛ぶ。	fly
キリンは首の長い動物である。	is
ラクダはたくさん水を飲まない。	drink
色を変えるクモもいる。	change
パンダは幸福をもたらす。	bring
その少年は2匹のテントウムシを捕まえた。	a couple of
この牛の群れは酪農生産に使用される。	This herd of
庭の池には魚の群れがいる。	a school of
羊飼いが羊の群れを放牧に連れ出す。	a flock of
狼の群れが森で見つかった。	A pack of

Birds fly.

The giraffe is an animal with a long neck.

Camels do not drink a lot of water.

Some spiders change colours.

Pandas bring us happiness.

The boy captured a couple of ladybirds.

This herd of cattle is used for dairy production.

There is a school of fish in the garden pond.

The shepherd takes a flock of sheep out to graze.

A pack of wolves was found in the woods.

3. Education (教育)

日本語	ヒント
ディスレクシアは学習障害である。	is
日本のほとんどの成人は読み書きができる。	are
私の学校には1,000人の生徒がいる。	has
すべての親は自由としつけの問題に直面する。	face
奨学金は学生に海外留学のチャンスを与える。	give
数学は英語と同じくらい重要である。	as important as
学生は働いている成人よりも自由度が高い。	have more freedom than
本を読めば読むほど、知識が増える。	The more / the more
知識があればあるほど、難易度は低くなる。	The more / the less
主題文は学術論文で最も重要な部分である。	the most important

Dyslexia is a learning disability.

Most adults in Japan are literate.

My school has 1,000 students.

All parents face the problems of freedom and discipline.

Scholarships give students a chance to study abroad.

Maths is as important as English.

Students have more freedom than working adults.

The more books you read, the more knowledge you will have.

The more knowledge you have, the less difficulty you will have.

The thesis statement is the most important part of an academic essay.

4. Science (科学)

DNA は存在する。	exists
ロボットは私たちの社会にとって有益である。	are
日本は技術的に進んだ国であった。	was
ソクラテスは哲学者であった。	was
インターネットは私たちに情報を与えてくれる。	gives
その理論は広く受け入れられている。	widely
そのデータは統計的に間違っている。	statistically
そのケースは徹底的に調査された。	thoroughly
情報の量は飛躍的に増えた。	exponentially
アインシュタインはほぼ間違いなく一番著名な科学者である。	arguably

DNA exists.

Robots are beneficial to our society.

Japan was a technologically advanced nation.

Socrates was a philosopher.

The internet gives us information.

The theory is widely accepted.

The data is statistically wrong.

The case was thoroughly investigated.

The amount of information grew exponentially.

Einstein is arguably the most eminent scientist.

5. Society (社会)

歴史は繰り返す。	repeats
日本人は人口密度の高い地域に住んでいる。	live
イスラム教がインドネシアでは主流の宗教である。	is
多くの国には新年を祝う伝統がある。	have
日本は国際的な役割を果たすべきである。	fulfil
飲酒は日本文化の重要な部分である。	important
戦争は人間の歴史に深い影響を及ぼす。	profound
マヤ族は驚くべき文化を発展させた。	remarkable
相互理解は世界平和に必要不可欠である。	indispensable
スコットランドの天気はとても変わりやすい。	changeable

History repeats itself.

Japanese people live in densely populated areas.

Islam is the dominant religion in Indonesia.

Many countries have the tradition of celebrating the new year.

Japan should fulfil its international role.

Drinking is an important part of Japanese culture.

War has a profound effect on human history.

The Maya developed a remarkable culture.

Mutual understanding is indispensable for world peace.

The weather in Scotland is very changeable.

6. Transport (交通)

私の夢はパイロットになることである。	is
飛行機は2時30分に離陸するでしょう。	take
ロンドン地下鉄は1863年に開業した。	began
大都市には多くの問題がある。	have
街の公共交通機関が生活を便利にしている。	makes
私たちの飛行機は2時間遅れた。	for
ヘリコプターについての議論が過熱している。	over
通勤者は渋滞を当たり前のことだと思っている。	for
事故はちょっとした不注意で引き起こされる。	about
東京からロンドンまでの距離は約9,600kmである。	from / to

My dream is to become a pilot.

The plane will take off at 2:30.

The London Underground began in 1863.

Big cities have a lot of problems.

Public transport in the city makes life convenient.

Our flight was delayed for two hours.

There is a growing controversy over helicopters.

Commuters take traffic jams for granted.

An accident is brought about by a bit of carelessness.

The distance from Tokyo to London is about 9,600 kilometers.

7. Health （健康）

ジョギングはとても人気がある。	is
美は永久ではない。	is not
肌は人の精神状態を反映する。	reflects
少々のアルコールは健康に良い。	is
マスクが感染のリスクを軽減する。	mitigate
その病気の原因が特定された。	was
さまざまな健康問題が議論された。	were
病院ではかなり多くの変更がなされた。	were made
医療は高額になり過ぎるべきではない。	should not be
乳幼児の食事は注意深く選ぶ必要がある。	need to be

Jogging is very popular.

Beauty is not permanent.

The skin reflects a person's mental state.

A little alcohol is good for your health.

Masks mitigate the risk of infection.

The cause of the disease was identified.

Various health issues were discussed.

Quite a few changes were made in the hospital.

Medical care should not be too expensive.

Infants' diets need to be carefully chosen.

8. Economy (経済)

金持ちの紳士がホテルに住んでいた。	lived
私のポケットから500円玉が滑り落ちた。	slipped
富は幸福を意味しない。	mean
私の父は高級レストランを経営している。	runs
日本は厳しい景気停滞に直面するだろう。	face
貧困で苦しむ人がたくさんいる。	who
ロンドンは人々の憧れの街として栄えた。	where
実家が金持ちの人はロンドンに住む余裕がある。	whose
富を生み出す職業はたくさんある。	that
一緒に住んでいる友人がもうすぐ引っ越す。	whom

A rich gentleman lived in a hotel.

A 500 yen coin slipped out of my pocket.

Wealth does not mean happiness.

My father runs a fancy restaurant.

Japan will face severe economic stagnation.

There are many people who suffer from poverty.

London was a prosperous city where people longed to live.

People whose parents are rich can afford to live in London.

There are many occupations that create wealth.

The friend with whom I live is moving out soon.

第**3**章

Task 1

Task 1の心得10選

・個人的な感想や評価は避ける

・グラフや図表から読み取れる情報のみを描写する

・150語以上、理想的には160語～200語で書く

・導入で指示文をパラフレーズ（paraphrasing）する

・文法の正確さ、特に時制と前置詞に注意する

・数字や期間などの表現は、繰り返しをなるべく避ける

・記号や略称、通称の使用は避ける

・増加や減少の描写では「型」をフル活用する

・小数点を含む数字や10未満の数字はスペルアウトする

・ダイアグラムよりグラフや図表の対策を優先する

Task 1

1 折れ線グラフの問題 Line Graph

The graph below shows the sales of four products sold at a certain sweet shop in 2023. Summarise the information by selecting and reporting the main features, and make comparisons where relevant.

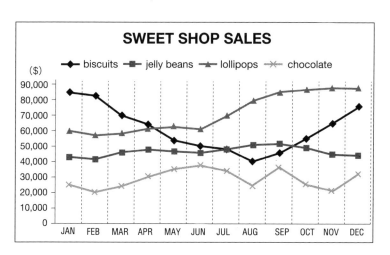

Brainstorming

Introduction▸ 指示文のパラフレーズと全体の描写をする
• respective monthly sales of four products
• all products experienced different changes

Body 1▸ 大きな変化をまとめる
• biscuits most popular in January, started to drop in the spring, reached a low in August
• lollipops second most popular in January, the stayed the same for the first half of the year but rose gradually after June

Body 2▸ 細かい変化をまとめる
• jelly beans about the same all year round
• chocolate the least popular product and fluctuated repeatedly

Conclusion▸ 上記を踏まえ全体をまとめる
• differences could be seen in the sales of each product
• some products' popularity changed according to the season while others stayed about the same all year

Model Essay

Introduction

This graph illustrates the respective monthly sales of four products at a sweet shop in the year 2023. Sales of each of these four products experienced different patterns of change over the course of one year.

Body 1

At the beginning of the year, biscuits were the most popular sweet and brought in around $85,000. However, sales started to drop in the springtime and reached a low of $40,000 in August. Lollipops were the second most purchased product in January and remained so until April. Although sales stayed about the same at around $60,000 for the first half of the year, they gradually rose in the latter half, making lollipops the most favoured product.

Body 2

The value of jelly beans sold did not experience any significant changes throughout the entire year, hovering between about $40,000 and $50,000. Chocolate was the least profitable product in 2023, and the sales fluctuated repeatedly between $20,000 and $37,000.

Conclusion

Overall, it can be seen that there was an apparent difference in the sales of all four products year-round. While some products' demand rose and fell according to the season, others experienced fewer seasonal changes.

(186 words)

Introduction

1 The graph below shows the sales of four products sold at a certain sweet shop in 2023. Summarise the information by selecting and reporting the main features, and make comparisons where relevant.

訳 下のグラフは、ある菓子店で販売されている4つの製品の2023年の売上を示している。主な特徴を選んで伝え、必要に応じて比較をしながら、情報をまとめなさい。

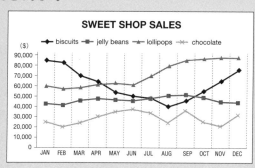

SWEET SHOP SALES

◆ biscuits ■ jelly beans ▲ lollipops ✕ chocolate

($)

90,000
80,000
70,000
60,000
50,000
40,000
30,000
20,000
10,000
0

JAN FEB MAR APR MAY JUN JUL AUG SEP OCT NOV DEC

 モデルエッセーより ||||||||||||||||||||||||||||||||||||||||||||||||||||||||||||||||||||||||||||||||||| |||||||||||||

This graph illustrates the respective monthly sales of four products at a sweet shop in the year 2023. Sales of each of these four products experienced different patterns of change over the course of one year.

訳 このグラフは、2023年のある菓子店での4つの製品それぞれの月間売上高を示している。これら4つの各製品の売上には、1年間にわたって異なるパターンの変化が見られた。

💬 respective の関連表現

This graph illustrates the respective monthly sales of four products at a sweet shop in the year 2023. で用いた respective には「それぞれの」という意味があり、通常、複数形を修飾する形容詞です。副詞の respectively（それぞれに）も IELTS のライティングで活用できる表現で、例えば Apples account for 10%. Bananas account for 20%. という2つの文を1つの文にして、Apples and bananas account for 10% and 20%, respectively.（リンゴとバナナはそれぞれ 10% と 20% を占めている）のように表現できます。ちなみに、名詞の respect には「尊敬」以外にも「点」という意味があり、in many respects（多くの点において）のように使えます。

▶ 解 説

指示文のパラフレーズ

▶ This graph illustrates the respective monthly sales of four products at a sweet shop in the year 2023.

　導入（Introduction）では、指示文の内容のパラフレーズをします。ここでは shows → illustrates、in 2023 → in the year 2023 のように言い換え、グラフが何を示しているのかを明確に1文で述べています。何を売っている店なのか、何年のデータなのかなど、指示文中に書かれている重要な要素が抜けてしまわないよう注意しながら簡潔にまとめましょう。

全体の描写

▶ Sales of each of these four products experienced different patterns of change over the course of one year.

　次にグラフから読み取れる全体的な傾向を簡潔に述べます。1つ1つの商品についての詳細な変化には言及せず、ここでは「4つの商品の売上には、1年間にわたって異なるパターンの変化が見られた」と全体描写をしています。

この**単語**、たいせつ！

- [ ] illustrate
  - ⑩例示する
- [ ] respective
  - ⑱それぞれの
- [ ] product
  - ⑧製品

この**フレーズ**、たいせつ！

- [ ] monthly sales
  - 月々の売上
- [ ] over the course of one year
  - 1年間にわたって

Body 1

1 The graph below shows the sales of four products sold at a certain sweet shop in 2023. Summarise the information by selecting and reporting the main features, and make comparisons where relevant.

訳 下のグラフは、ある菓子店で販売されている4つの製品の2023年の売上を示している。主な特徴を選んで伝え、必要に応じて比較をしながら、情報をまとめなさい。

SWEET SHOP SALES

◆ biscuits ■ jelly beans ▲ lollipops ✕ chocolate

🔍 **モデルエッセーより** ||||||||||||||||||||||||||||||||||||||||||||||||||||||||| |||||||||||||

At the beginning of the year, biscuits were the most popular sweet and brought in around $85,000. However, sales started to drop in the springtime and reached a low of $40,000 in August. Lollipops were the second most purchased product in January and remained so until April. Although sales stayed about the same at around $60,000 for the first half of the year, they gradually rose in the latter half, making lollipops the most favoured product.

訳 年の初めにはビスケットが最も人気の菓子で、およそ85,000ドルの売上をもたらした。しかし、春に売上は落ち込み始め、8月に40,000ドルの低さにまで達した。ロリポップは1月に2番目に多く購入された製品で、その順位は4月まで続いた。この年の上半期の売上はおよそ60,000ドルでほぼ一定であったが、下半期に売上は少しずつ上昇し、ロリポップは一番人気の製品になった。

解 説

ビスケットの売上の変化

▶ At the beginning of the year, biscuits were the most popular sweet and brought in around $85,000. However, sales started to drop in the springtime and reached a low of $40,000 in August.

本論1（Body 1）ではグラフの中に見られる大きな変化について描写していきます。ここでは「年の初めにビスケットが最も人気だったが、春に売上が落ちた」ことを、下線部やハイライト部分のように明確な時期と具体的な数値を挙げて比較しつつ示しています。最も売上が高いことについて、the most popular（最も人気がある）とグラフにはない言葉で表現していますが、主観的な意見や見解ではなく客観的な事実の表現ですから問題ありません。

ロリポップの売上の変化

▶ Lollipops were the second most purchased product in January and remained so until April. Although sales stayed about the same at around $60,000 for the first half of the year, they gradually rose in the latter half, making lollipops the most favoured product.

時系列順に売上の変化を示す際には、ただ「〇月は〜」と月の名前を挙げていくだけではなく、下線部のような多様な言い回しで時間の変化を示せるようにしましょう。また、売上の具体的な数値をすべて書くことは難しいので、顕著なものを抽出して書く必要があります。ここでも、具体的な数値や他の製品との比較を組み込みましょう。

この**単語**、たいせつ！

- [ ] drop
  ⟨動⟩落ちる
- [ ] reach
  ⟨動⟩達する
- [ ] remain
  ⟨動⟩〜のままである

この**フレーズ**、たいせつ！

- [ ] bring in
  （利益を）生ずる
- [ ] stay about the same
  ほぼ同じままである
- [ ] for the first half of the year
  最初の半年間
- [ ] gradually rise
  徐々に上がる
- [ ] the most favoured product
  最も好まれた製品

Body 2

1 The graph below shows the sales of four products sold at a certain sweet shop in 2023. Summarise the information by selecting and reporting the main features, and make comparisons where relevant.

訳 下のグラフは、ある菓子店で販売されている4つの製品の2023年の売上を示している。主な特徴を選んで伝え、必要に応じて比較をしながら、情報をまとめなさい。

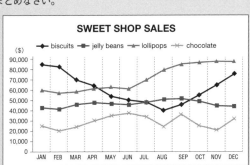

 モデルエッセーより ||||||||||||||||||||||||||||||||||||||||||||||||||||||||||||||||||||||||||||| |||||||||||||||

The value of jelly beans sold did not experience any significant changes throughout the entire year, hovering between about $40,000 and $50,000. Chocolate was the least profitable product in 2023, and the sales fluctuated repeatedly between $20,000 and $37,000.

訳 ジェリービーンズの売上額は1年全体を通しておよそ40,000ドルと50,000ドルの間で推移し、あまり大きな変化は見られなかった。チョコレートは、2023年で最も収益が低い製品で、その売上は20,000ドルと37,000ドルの間で繰り返し変動した。

💬 時期や期間の表現

時系列順に数値の変化を書く際には、以下のようなフレーズを活用しましょう。

in the spring（春に）
all through the year（1年中）
in the first half of the year（最初の半年で）
throughout the entire year（年間を通して）
at the beginning of the year（1年の始まりに）

within the next three months
　（次の3カ月以内に）
during the next three months（次の3カ月間で）
over the course of three years（3年間で）
over the past three years（過去3年間で）

▶ 解 説

ジェリービーンズの売上の変化

▶ The value of jelly beans sold did not experience any significant changes throughout the entire year, hovering between about $40,000 and $50,000.

本論2（Body 2）では、グラフ中に見られる細かな変化について描写していきます。ここでは、年間を通してあまり売上に大きな変化が見られなかったジェリービーンズについて、具体的な数字を示しています。

チョコレートの売上の変化

▶ Chocolate was the least profitable product in 2023, and the sales fluctuated repeatedly between $20,000 and $37,000.

次も同様に、具体的な数字を用いて、チョコレートが最も収益が低く、変動を繰り返したことを描写しています。下線部のthe least profitableやfluctuated repeatedlyのような高度な表現を用いるのがポイントです。

 「数値変化の少なさ」の表現

数値の変化が少ないことを述べた後、ここでのように最高値と最低値を具体的に挙げ、それらの2つの数値の間で動いていることに触れると分かりやすくなります。ここで使われている not experience any significant changes 以外に、次のような表現も良いでしょう。

stay the same（同じままでいる）
stay unchanged（変わらないままである）
remain unvaried（変化せずにいる）
remain largely unchanged（大きく変化せずにいる）

Conclusion

1 The graph below shows the sales of four products sold at a certain sweet shop in 2023. Summarise the information by selecting and reporting the main features, and make comparisons where relevant.

訳 下のグラフは、ある菓子店で販売されている4つの製品の2023年の売上を示している。主な特徴を選んで伝え、必要に応じて比較をしながら、情報をまとめなさい。

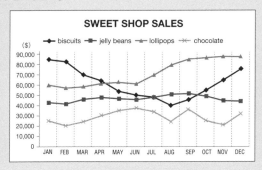

SWEET SHOP SALES

($) ◆ biscuits ■ jelly beans ▲ lollipops ✕ chocolate

JAN FEB MAR APR MAY JUN JUL AUG SEP OCT NOV DEC

🔍 モデルエッセーより ||||||||||||||||||||||||||||||||||||||||||||||||||||||||||||||| ||||||||||||||

Overall, it can be seen that there was an apparent difference in the sales of all four products year-round. While some products' demand rose and fell according to the season, others experienced fewer seasonal changes.

訳 全体的に見ると、1年を通し、全部で4つの製品の売上には明らかな違いがあったことが分かる。一部の製品の需要は季節ごとに増減が見られたが、季節ごとに大きな違いが見られなかった製品もある。

 客観的な表現

IELTS のライティングでは主観的な表現は厳禁です。It can be ... を用いることで客観性を高めることができますが、冗長にもなり得るので注意しましょう。

It can be seen that ～（～ということが分かる）
It can be observed that ～（～ということが観察できる）
It can be argued that ～（～ということが主張できる）
It can be recognised that ～（～ということが認められる）

解説

全体の描写

▶ Overall, it can be seen that there was an apparent difference in the sales of all four products year-round. While some products' demand rose and fell according to the season, others experienced fewer seasonal changes.

　結論（Conclusion）では、導入（Introduction）よりもさらに具体的に全体をまとめて描写します。概観すると年間を通し各要素にどのような変化が見られたのかを簡潔にまとめています。下線部のようなディスコースマーカー（discourse markers）を用い、本論1（Body 1）と本論2（Body 2）の内容に沿って、全体的に年間を通して各製品に売上の違いが見られたことを述べるようにしましょう。Task 1は最低でも150語以上書く必要がありますが、本論（Body）で文字数を稼げる場合、結論（Conclusion）のパラグラフは不要です。

この**単語**、たいせつ！

☐ overall
　㊀全体として
☐ year-round
　㊀年間を通して
☐ demand
　㊂需要

この**フレーズ**、たいせつ！

☐ apparent difference
　明らかな違い
☐ rise and fall
　増減する
☐ seasonal changes
　季節ごとの変化

📖 折れ線グラフの問題で使えるコロケーション

☐ fall gradually
　徐々に下がる
☐ a dramatic increase
　劇的な増加
☐ show a sharp increase
　激しい増加を見せる
☐ decrease by 20%
　20％減る
☐ remain stable
　安定したままである

☐ reach a peak
　ピークに達する
☐ reach a plateau
　停滞期に達する
☐ fluctuate repeatedly
　繰り返し変動する
☐ a noticeable trend
　顕著な傾向
☐ a substantial increase
　かなりの増加

Task 1

2 円グラフの問題 Pie Chart

The pie charts below show the respective percentages of men and women who ordered each of five different types of sandwiches at a certain sandwich shop. Summarise the information by selecting and reporting the main features, and make comparisons where relevant.

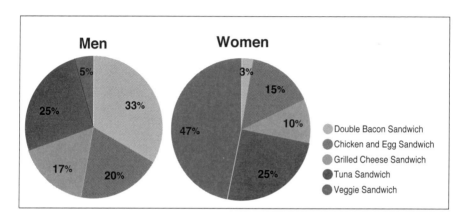

Brainstorming

Introduction ▶ 指示文のパラフレーズと全体の描写をする
- difference in sandwich choice based on gender
- preference of some sandwiches differs greatly by gender, others show less difference

Body 1 ▶ 大きな違いをまとめる
- Double Bacon Sandwich was the most popular order among men
- Veggie Sandwich was the most popular among women

Body 2 ▶ 細かい違いをまとめる
- Chicken and Egg Sandwich and Grilled Cheese Sandwich slightly more popular among men
- Tuna Sandwich equally popular

Conclusion ▶ 上記を踏まえ全体をまとめる
- big difference in preference of Double Bacon Sandwich and Veggie Sandwich
- other sandwiches not much of a difference

Model Essay

Introduction

The two pie charts reveal the difference in sandwich choice based on gender. It can be observed that while the preference for some sandwiches differs greatly by gender, the difference is less obvious in others.

Body 1

The Double Bacon Sandwich was the most popular order among men, with 33% of male customers ordering it. In contrast, only 3% of women had a preference for this sandwich. Among female customers, the Veggie Sandwich was by far the most popular, since nearly half of them ordered this sandwich. However, only 5% of men chose to eat this sandwich.

Body 2

The popularity of the Chicken and Egg Sandwich and the Grilled Cheese Sandwich was slightly higher among men than among women. The Tuna Sandwich was equally popular among both genders, at 25%.

Conclusion

Although there was a significant gender difference in the percentage of people who ordered the Double Bacon Sandwich and those who ordered the Veggie Sandwich, the other three types of sandwiches did not show such a big difference.

(165 words)

Introduction

2 The pie charts below show the respective percentages of men and women who ordered each of five different types of sandwiches at a certain sandwich shop. Summarise the information by selecting and reporting the main features, and make comparisons where relevant.

訳 下の円グラフは、あるサンドイッチ店で5種類の各サンドイッチを注文した男性と女性それぞれの割合を示している。主な特徴を選んで伝え、必要に応じて比較をしながら、情報をまとめなさい。

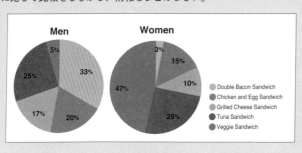

 モデルエッセーより ||||||||||||||||||||||||||||||||||||||||||||||||||||||||||||||||||||||||||||||||||||||||

The two pie charts reveal the difference in sandwich choice based on gender. It can be observed that while the preference for some sandwiches differs greatly by gender, the difference is less obvious in others.

訳 この2つの円グラフは、性別によってサンドイッチの選択がどう変わるかを明らかにしている。性別ごとに好みが大きく分かれるサンドイッチの種類もあれば、（好みの）差があまり明白でないものもあることが見て取れる。

💬 **指示文のパラフレーズに使える表現**

Task 1 の導入（Introduction）では、指示文をパラフレーズする必要があります。モデルエッセーでは The pie charts below show ... を、「明らかにする」という意味の reveal を用いて The two pie charts reveal ... と言い換えていますが、他にも indicate（指し示す）、represent（示す）、illustrate（例示する）、demonstrate（実証する）などの動詞を使って言い換え可能です。

解 説

指示文のパラフレーズ

▶ The two pie charts reveal the difference in sandwich choice based on <u>gender</u>.

　導入（Introduction）では、指示文のパラフレーズをします。このグラフの場合、各サンドイッチを買った人の割合を男女別に示しているので、2つの軸が存在することを明示しましょう。下線部のように、men and women を gender に言い換える方法があります。

全体の描写

▶ It can be observed that while the preference for some sandwiches differs greatly by gender, the difference is less obvious in others.

　この導入では、グラフに示された詳細な情報には触れず、全体から読み取れる概要的な内容を述べています。日本人英語学習者は there is や there are を多用しがちですが、There is a less obvious difference. ではなく、ハイライト部分のように the difference is less obvious と表現するようにしましょう。

この単語、たいせつ！

- [ ] reveal
  - (動)明らかにする
- [ ] gender
  - (名)性別
- [ ] preference
  - (名)好み
- [ ] obvious
  - (形)明らかな

このフレーズ、たいせつ！

- [ ] differ greatly
  - 大きく異なる

Body 1

2 The pie charts below show the respective percentages
of men and women who ordered each of five different types
of sandwiches at a certain sandwich shop. Summarise the
information by selecting and reporting the main features, and
make comparisons where relevant.

訳 下の円グラフは、あるサンドイッチ店で5種類の各サンドイッチを注文
した男性と女性それぞれの割合を示している。主な特徴を選んで伝え、必
要に応じて比較をしながら、情報をまとめなさい。

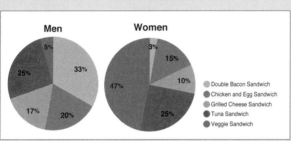

モデルエッセーより |||||||||||||||||||||||||||||||||||||||||||||||||||||||||||||||||||||||||||| |||||||||||

The Double Bacon Sandwich was the most popular order among
men, with 33% of male customers ordering it. In contrast, only 3% of
women had a preference for this sandwich. Among female customers,
the Veggie Sandwich was by far the most popular, since nearly half of
them ordered this sandwich. However, only 5% of men chose to eat
this sandwich.

訳 Double Bacon Sandwich は男性の間で最も人気があり、男性客の33%がこれを注文し
た。それとは対照的に、女性の3%しかこのサンドイッチを好まなかった。女性客の間では
Veggie Sandwich が圧倒的に人気が高く、半数近くがこのサンドイッチを注文した。しか
し、男性客の5%しかこのサンドイッチを選ばなかった。

▶ 解説

Double Bacon Sandwich について

▶ The Double Bacon Sandwich was the most popular order among men, with 33% of male customers ordering it. In contrast, only 3% of women had a preference for this sandwich.

　本論1（Body 1）ではグラフ中に見られる大きな違いを描写しています。ここでは男性客と女性客で人気に大きな差があったDouble Bacon Sandwich と Veggie Sandwich について述べています。各サンドイッチを男女がそれぞれどれくらいの割合で購入したのか、ディスコースマーカー（discourse markers）を用いて比較し、ハイライト部分のように具体的な数値を挙げながら描写しましょう。

Veggie Sandwich について

▶ Among female customers, the Veggie Sandwich was by far the most popular, since nearly half of them ordered this sandwich. However, only 5% of men chose to eat this sandwich.

　ここでもディスコースマーカーを用いて、2つの要素を比較しながら描写しています。また、具体的な数値を挙げる際には円グラフの数値をそのまま引用するのではなく、1つ目のハイライト部分のように言葉で割合を示すといった方法も用い、表現にバラエティを持たせましょう。

 対比のディスコースマーカー

論理性のある文章を書くには、ディスコースマーカー（discourse markers）を適切に使用する必要があります。モデルエッセイでは In contrast（対照的に）と However（しかしながら）を用いて男性と女性の対比をしています。2つの要素の対比には、以下のような表現を覚えておくと便利です。

however（しかしながら）
whereas（一方で）
meanwhile（一方で）
conversely（逆に）
in contrast（対照的に）

contrary to A（A とは反対に）
compared to A（A と比較すると）
on the contrary（それどころか）
in comparison with A（A と比較して）
on the other hand（一方で）

Body 2

2 The pie charts below show the respective percentages of men and women who ordered each of five different types of sandwiches at a certain sandwich shop. Summarise the information by selecting and reporting the main features, and make comparisons where relevant.

訳 下の円グラフは、あるサンドイッチ店で5種類の各サンドイッチを注文した男性と女性それぞれの割合を示している。主な特徴を選んで伝え、必要に応じて比較をしながら、情報をまとめなさい。

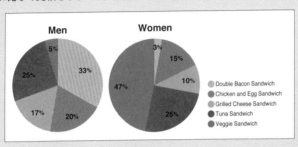

Men   Women

- Double Bacon Sandwich
- Chicken and Egg Sandwich
- Grilled Cheese Sandwich
- Tuna Sandwich
- Veggie Sandwich

 モデルエッセーより |||||||||||||||||||||||||||||||||||||||||||||||||||||||||||||||||||||||

The popularity of the Chicken and Egg Sandwich and the Grilled Cheese Sandwich was slightly higher among men than among women. The Tuna Sandwich was equally popular among both genders, at 25%.

訳 Chicken and Egg Sandwich と Grilled Cheese Sandwich は女性よりも男性の間での人気が少し高かった。Tuna Sandwich はともに25%であり、男女間で等しく人気であった。

💬 Task 1 で使える副詞

IELTS のライティング Task 1 で高得点を狙うには、副詞の使用が重要です。モデルエッセーでは slightly や equally を効果的に用いています。以下のようなアカデミックライティングにふさわしい副詞を、相性の良い動詞とともに意識的に覚えていきましょう。

gradually（徐々に）
steadily（着実に）
completely（完全に）
dramatically（劇的に）
drastically（大々的に）

considerably（かなり）
significantly（顕著に）
substantially（相当に）
exponentially（急に）
marginally（わずかに）

解 説

Chicken and Egg Sandwich と Grilled Cheese Sandwich について

▶ The popularity of the Chicken and Egg Sandwich and the Grilled Cheese Sandwich was <u>slightly higher</u> among men than among women.

　本論2（Body 2）では、あまり大きな違いが見られないものについて描写しています。わずかな違いがあったことを、下線部のように程度を表す副詞を用いて表現しました。

Tuna Sandwich について

▶ The Tuna Sandwich was <u>equally</u> popular among both genders, at 25%.

　男性客と女性客の間で違いが見られなかったTuna Sandwichについて、下線部の「同等に」を表す副詞を用いて描写しています。ハイライト部分では、具体的な数字を、「数値の1点」を表す前置詞のatで示しています。

倍数の表現

数値の示し方には、具体的な数字をそのまま示す方法以外に、倍数表現を用いて示す方法もあります。文章中では繰り返しを避け、多様な表現を使用しましょう。

The number of A is half of B. （A の数は B の半分である）
The number of A halved in 2020. （A の数は 2020 年に半分になった）
The number of A is one third of B. （A の数は B の 3 分の 1 である）
The number of A is one quarter of B. （A の数は B の 4 分の 1 である）
The number of A is one fifth of B. （A の数は B の 5 分の 1 である）
The number of A is three quarters of B. （A の数は B の 4 分の 3 である）
A is double the number of B. （A は B の 2 倍の数である）
The number of A increased twofold. （A の数は 2 倍に増えた）
The number of A doubled over the past decade. （A の数は過去 10 年で 2 倍になった）
The number of A tripled over the past decade. （A の数は過去 10 年で 3 倍になった）
The number of A increased threefold. （A の数は 3 倍に増えた）
The number of A is quadruple that of B. （A の数は B の 4 倍である）
The number of A is five times more than that of B. （A の数は B の 5 倍である）
The number of A increased ninefold. （A の数は 9 倍に増えた）
The number of A increased almost sevenfold. （A の数はほぼ 7 倍に増えた）

Conclusion

2 The pie charts below show the respective percentages of men and women who ordered each of five different types of sandwiches at a certain sandwich shop. Summarise the information by selecting and reporting the main features, and make comparisons where relevant.

訳 下の円グラフは、あるサンドイッチ店で5種類の各サンドイッチを注文した男性と女性それぞれの割合を示している。主な特徴を選んで伝え、必要に応じて比較をしながら、情報をまとめなさい。

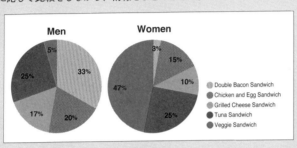

 モデルエッセーより ||||||||||||||||||||||||||||||||||||||||||||||||||||||||||||||||||||||||||||||||||| |||||||||||

Although there was a significant gender difference in the percentage of people who ordered the Double Bacon Sandwich and those who ordered the Veggie Sandwich, the other three types of sandwiches did not show such a big difference.

訳 Double Bacon Sandwich を注文した人の割合と Veggie Sandwich を注文した人の割合には、性別により大きな差があったが、他の3種類のサンドイッチにはそれほど大きな差が見られなかった。

割合の表し方

割合を意味する percentage と proportion と ratio の使い方を押さえましょう。
percentage の cent が「100」を意味することから、percentage は 0% ～ 100% の割合を示す言葉であると分かります。5% = one in twenty、10% = one in ten、25% = a quarter、50% = a half、66% = two thirds、70% = seven in ten、75% = three quarters、80% = four fifths のようにパラフレーズできるようにしておきましょう。
proportion は「全体に対しての一部分」について用い、A small proportion of chimpanzees preferred apples.（チンパンジーのごく一部がリンゴを好んだ）のように全体の中での比率関係を描写できます。ratio はある2つの比率を比べる際に使われることが多い語です。teacher-student ratio（教師と生徒の比率）のようなフレーズで覚えておくと良いでしょう。

解 説

全体の描写

▶ Although there was a significant gender difference in the percentage of people who ordered the Double Bacon Sandwich and those who ordered the Veggie Sandwich, the other three types of sandwiches did not show such a big difference.

結論（Conclusion）では、ここまでの内容を踏まえて、全体をまとめ、締めくくります。ここでは、本論1（Body 1）と本論2（Body 2）の内容に沿って、まず男女の間で好みの大きく分かれたサンドイッチについて、次にあまり大きな違いが見られなかったサンドイッチについて、それぞれ簡潔にまとめ、1文で述べています。

このフレーズ、たいせつ!

- gender difference
  性別ごとの差

📖 円グラフの問題で使えるコロケーション

- by far the most popular
  圧倒的に人気のある
- equally popular
  同じくらい人気のある
- the second most popular
  2番目に人気のある
- the least popular of all
  すべての中で最も人気のない
- a majority of A
  Aの大多数
- almost the same
  ほとんど同じ
- nearly double
  ほぼ2倍になる
- nearly a third of A
  Aのほぼ3分の1
- make up almost half
  半分近くを占める
- account for A
  Aを占める

Task 1

3 棒グラフの問題 Bar Graph

The bar graph below shows what kind of pets the students in a certain first grade class own and the respective number of students who own each type of animal. Summarise the information by selecting and reporting the main features, and make comparisons where relevant.

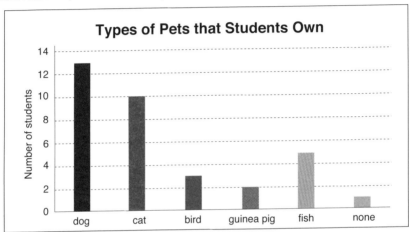

☆Brainstorming

Introduction 指示文のパラフレーズと全体の描写をする
- number of students in a certain first grade class who own various kinds of pets
- students own various types of pets but some are more common than others

Body 1 数値の大きいものをまとめる
- dogs are the most popular: 13
- cats are next: 10
- these two are much more popular than the others

Body 2 数値の小さいものをまとめる
- birds and guinea pigs are about the same
- fish are a little bit more popular
- only one student did not own any pets

Conclusion 上記を踏まえ全体をまとめる
- some pets are more popular than others
- difference in the number of students who own each pet

Model Essay

Introduction

The data in the bar graph displays the number of students in a certain first grade class who own various kinds of pets. It can be seen that the students in this class own several different types of pets, but some animals are more common than others.

Body 1

By far the most popular are dogs, since 13 students in the entire class own one. The second most popular pets are cats, and 10 students replied that they have a cat at home. The number of students that own cats and dogs combined accounts for approximately two thirds of all the pet owners in this class. These two animals are much more popular than the other three pets.

Body 2

Fish are the third most popular, and birds come in fourth. Since only two students have guinea pigs, this makes them the least preferred pet of them all. Only one student answered that they do not have any pets.

Conclusion

In summary, it can be said that the popularity of each pet differs greatly and while some of these animals are owned by a larger proportion of students, others are only owned by a handful.

(190 words)

Introduction

3 The bar graph below shows what kind of pets the students in a certain first grade class own and the respective number of students who own each type of animal. Summarise the information by selecting and reporting the main features, and make comparisons where relevant.

訳 下の棒グラフは、ある小学校1年生のクラスの生徒がどのようなペットを飼っているか、またそれぞれの種類のペットを何人の生徒が飼っているのかを示している。主な特徴を選んで伝え、必要に応じて比較をしながら、情報をまとめなさい。

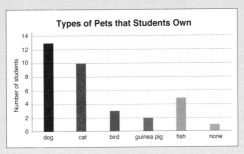

Types of Pets that Students Own

 モデルエッセーより ||||||||||||||||||||||||||||||||||||||||||||||||||||||||||||||||||||||||| ||||||||||||

The data in the bar graph displays the number of students in a certain first grade class who own various kinds of pets. It can be seen that the students in this class own several different types of pets, but some animals are more common than others.

訳 この棒グラフのデータは、ある小学校1年生のクラスにおいて、さまざまな種類のペットを飼っている生徒の人数を示している。このクラスの生徒は数種類のペットを飼っているが、他よりよく飼われている動物も存在することが分かる。

certain の使い方

certain は限定用法の形容詞として「ある〜」という意味でよく使われ、指示文にも a certain first grade class（ある小学校1年生のクラス）という表現が出てきます。certain には「いくらかの」という意味もあり、to a certain degree（ある程度まで）という表現も頻出です。

▶ 解説

指示文のパラフレーズ

▶ The data in the bar graph displays the number of
students in a certain first grade class who own
various kinds of pets.

導入（Introduction）では指示文のパラフレーズをしま
す。下線部では、The bar graph below を The data in the
bar graph と言い換えています。

全体の描写

▶ It can be seen that the students in this class own
several different types of pets, but some animals
are more common than others.

ここでは、グラフに示された詳細な情報は組み込まず
に、全体から読み取れる概要的な内容を描写しています。
各ペットを飼っている人数などには触れずに、「クラスの
生徒は数種類のペットを飼っているが、よく飼われている
ペットとそうでないペットがいる」ことを述べています。
It can be ... を用いることで客観性を高めることができま
すが、冗長になってしまわないように注意しましょう。

Body 1

3 The bar graph below shows what kind of pets the students in a certain first grade class own and the respective number of students who own each type of animal. Summarise the information by selecting and reporting the main features, and make comparisons where relevant.

訳 下の棒グラフは、ある小学校1年生のクラスの生徒がどのようなペットを飼っているか、またそれぞれの種類のペットを何人の生徒が飼っているのかを示している。主な特徴を選んで伝え、必要に応じて比較をしながら、情報をまとめなさい。

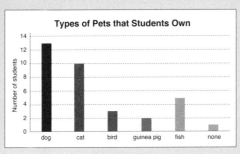

Types of Pets that Students Own

 モデルエッセーより ||||||||||||||||||||||||||||||||||||||||||||||||||||||||||||||||| |||||||||||||||||

By far the most popular are dogs, since 13 students in the entire class own one. The second most popular pets are cats, and 10 students replied that they have a cat at home. The number of students that own cats and dogs combined accounts for approximately two thirds of all the pet owners in this class. These two animals are much more popular than the other three pets.

訳 クラス全体で13人の生徒が飼っていて、圧倒的に人気があるのが犬である。次に人気が高いペットは猫であり、10人の生徒が家に猫がいると答えた。犬か猫を飼っている生徒の合計人数は、クラスでペットを飼っている生徒全員の約3分の2を占めている。これら2種類の動物は、他の3種類よりもはるかに人気がある。

account for の意味と使い方

account for A は「Aを説明する」「Aの原因である」「Aを占める」などの意味を持ち、Task 1で使える重要表現です。In IELTS, grammar accounts for 25% of the marks in your writing test. （IELTS では、文法がライティングの採点の 25% を占めている）のような使い方ができます。

解説

人気のあるペット

▶ By far the most popular are dogs, since <u>13 students</u> in the entire class own one. The second most popular pets are cats, and <u>10 students</u> replied that they have a cat at home. The number of students that own cats and dogs combined accounts for approximately two thirds of all the pet owners in this class. These two animals are much more popular than the other three pets.

　本論1（Body 1）で人気のあるペットについて、本論2（Body 2）で人気のないペットについて描写しています。本論1では、他のペットと比べて飼っている生徒数が著しく多い犬と猫について、下線部のように具体的な数値を交えながら人気順に描写しています。さらにハイライト部分では、この2つのペットを飼っている人数の多さを示すために、犬か猫を飼っている生徒数を合わせるとクラス全体でペットを飼っている生徒数の約3分の2を占めると述べています。

決まり文句に注意

猫が雨を降らせ犬が風を起こす、という北欧神話に由来するとされるrain like cats and dogs（雨が激しく降る）という表現を聞いたことがあるでしょうか? busy as a bee（とても忙しい）や reinvent the wheel（一からやり直す）など、日常会話やビジネスのやりとりで頻繁に遭遇する表現があります。これらや、at the end of the day（最終的には）、in a nutshell（簡単に言えば）などは、日本人の英語学習者が文章にもよく使用してしまう表現です。こうした決まり文句（cliché）やことわざ（proverb）は、アカデミックライティングでは使わないよう注意しましょう。

この単語、たいせつ!

☐ reply
　働回答する
☐ combine
　働組み合わせる

このフレーズ、たいせつ!

☐ entire class
　クラス全体
☐ account for A
　Aを占める
☐ approximately two thirds
　おおよそ3分の2

Body 2

3 The bar graph below shows what kind of pets the students in a certain first grade class own and the respective number of students who own each type of animal. Summarise the information by selecting and reporting the main features, and make comparisons where relevant.

訳 下の棒グラフは、ある小学校1年生のクラスの生徒がどのようなペットを飼っているか、またそれぞれの種類のペットを何人の生徒が飼っているのかを示している。主な特徴を選んで伝え、必要に応じて比較をしながら、情報をまとめなさい。

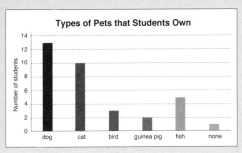

Types of Pets that Students Own

モデルエッセーより |||||||||||||||||||||||||||||||||||||||||||||||||||||||||||||||||||||| |||||||||||||||

Fish are the third most popular, and birds come in fourth. Since only two students have guinea pigs, this makes them the least preferred pet of them all. Only one student answered that they do not have any pets.

訳 3番目に人気が高いのが魚で、鳥が4位である。2人の生徒しかモルモットを飼っていないので、(モルモットは) 全体の中で最も人気のないペットということになる。1人の生徒のみが、ペットを何も飼っていないと答えた。

💬 come を使った「順位」の表し方

come in は、競馬などで「入賞する」を表す言い回しで、そこから「順位が (序列の) ～位になる」という意味で使われるようになりました。The team came in fifth. (そのチームは5位になった) のように使うことができます。come top は「1位になる」を意味し、The team came top of the chart. (そのチームはグラフで1位になった) のように使えます。

解 説

人気のないペット

▶ Fish are the third most popular, and birds come in fourth. Since only two students have guinea pigs, this makes them the least preferred pet of them all. Only one student answered that they do not have any pets.

　本論2（Body 2）では人気のあまりないペットについて描写しています。つまり、本論1（Body 1）では触れなかった他の3種類のペットについて、下線部のような表現を用いて、人気のある順に挙げています。そして最後に、ペットを飼っていない生徒の人数について触れています。

この単語、たいせつ！

☐ prefer
　動 好む

このフレーズ、たいせつ！

☐ the third most popular
　3番目に人気のある
☐ come in fourth
　4位になる

綴りを間違えやすい単語

IELTS のライティングでは、英単語の正確な綴りが求められます。また、イギリス英語とアメリカ英語を交ぜて使うと減点対象となります。ここでは、私が教える大学の授業で日本人英語学習者が実際にスペリングを間違えた英単語を紹介します。

weird（変な）
muscle（筋肉）
foreign（外国の）
leisure（余暇）
rhythm（リズム）
deceive（だます）
January（1月）
privilege（特権）
exercise（運動）
amateur（アマチュア）
medieval（中世の）
discipline（規律）
grammar（文法）
professor（教授）

ingenious（巧妙な）
miniature（ミニチュア）
irrelevant（関係のない）
influential（影響力のある）
noticeable（目立つ）
guarantee（保証）
embarrass（恥ずかしがらせる）
catastrophe（大災害）
anonymous（匿名の）
government（政府）
maintenance（維持）
entrepreneur（起業家）
questionnaire（アンケート）
accommodate（収容する）

Conclusion

3 The bar graph below shows what kind of pets the students in a certain first grade class own and the respective number of students who own each type of animal. Summarise the information by selecting and reporting the main features, and make comparisons where relevant.

訳 下の棒グラフは、ある小学校1年生のクラスの生徒がどのようなペットを飼っているか、またそれぞれの種類のペットを何人の生徒が飼っているのかを示している。主な特徴を選んで伝え、必要に応じて比較をしながら、情報をまとめなさい。

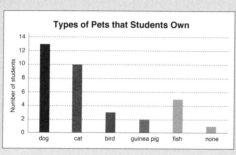

モデルエッセーより ||||||||||||||||||||||||||||||||||||||||||||||||||||||||||||||||||||||||| |||||||||||||

In summary, it can be said that the popularity of each pet differs greatly and while some of these animals are owned by a larger proportion of students, others are only owned by a handful.

訳 まとめると、それぞれのペットの人気は大きく異なっていると言える。そして大きな割合の生徒に飼われている動物もいれば、一握りの生徒にしか飼われていない動物もいる。

▶ 解 説

全体の描写

▶ In summary, it can be said that the popularity of each pet differs greatly and while some of these animals are owned by a larger proportion of students, others are only owned by a handful.

　導入（Introduction）の後半で述べた内容をより具体化して全体を描写していきます。そこでは、「クラスの生徒は数種類のペットを飼っているが、よく飼われているペットとそうでないペットがいる」ということを伝えましたが、ここでは、それを別の表現で書くとともに、どれくらいの生徒たちに飼われているのかについて述べています。

📖 棒グラフの問題で使えるコロケーション

☐ the previous year
　前の年
☐ a period of five weeks
　5週間の期間
☐ the least amount
　最も少ない量
☐ significant difference
　顕著な違い
☐ as opposed to A
　Aとは反対に

☐ a gradual decrease
　段階的な減少
☐ increase dramatically
　劇的に増える
☐ drop rapidly
　急に落ちる
☐ show an increase
　増加を見せる
☐ decline steadily
　着実に減少する

Task 1

4 表の問題 Table

The table below indicates the number of times that 15-year-old school students in China, Korea, Japan, and Taiwan study four different subjects per week. Summarise the information by selecting and reporting the main features, and make comparisons where relevant.

	Maths	Science	English	History
China	6	3	10	4
Korea	5	6	12	2
Japan	8	5	7	3
Taiwan	5	6	10	3

Brainstorming

Introduction 指示文のパラフレーズと全体の描写をする
- differences in the number of classes 15-year-old students take every week
- some subjects show a greater difference in how much time students spend on studying them

Body 1 違いが比較的大きい教科について
- English shows the biggest difference: most Korea, least Japan
- maths shows a bit of a difference: most Japan

Body 2 違いが比較的小さい教科について
- science shows a slight difference: top countries Korea and Taiwan, lowest China
- history has the least difference: each country studies it for two to four hours per week

Model Essay

Introduction

The table indicates the differences in the number of maths, science, English and history classes that 15-year-old students take every week at school in four East Asian countries. While the amount of time that some subjects are studied differs greatly, others show less of a difference.

Body 1

Schools invest the most time in teaching students English in all of the four countries except Japan. Korea takes the lead at 12 hours per week, while China and Taiwan tie in second place. However, in Japan, students only study English for seven classes every week, which is only a little more than half the time that Korean students spend. On the other hand, Japanese students spend eight classes learning maths, which is more than in any other country. Korea and Taiwan do not seem to be as enthusiastic about this subject since they only require students to study it for five classes.

Body 2

There is only a slight difference in the amount of time used for studying science. The top countries are Korea and Taiwan at six classes per week, whereas the lowest is China at three classes. The subject which is most equally emphasised in all four countries is history, since each dedicates two to four classes every week to this subject.

(209 words)

Introduction

4 The table below indicates the number of times that 15-year-old school students in China, Korea, Japan, and Taiwan study four different subjects per week. Summarise the information by selecting and reporting the main features, and make comparisons where relevant.

訳 下の表は、中国、韓国、日本、台湾の15歳の生徒が、4種類の教科を1週間に学ぶ時間数を示している。主な特徴を選んで伝え、必要に応じて比較をしながら、情報をまとめなさい。

	Maths	Science	English	History
China	6	3	10	4
Korea	5	6	12	2
Japan	8	5	7	3
Taiwan	5	6	10	3

 モデルエッセーより ||||||||||||||||||||||||||||||||||||||||||||||||||||||||||||||||||||||||||||| ||||||||||||

The table indicates the differences in the number of maths, science, English and history classes that 15-year-old students take every week at school in four East Asian countries. While the amount of time that some subjects are studied differs greatly, others show less of a difference.

訳 この表は、4つの東アジアの国で15歳の生徒が毎週学校で受けている数学、理科、英語、歴史の授業数の違いを示している。学ぶ時間に大きな違いがある教科もあれば、そこまでの違いが見られない教科もある。

💬 さまざまな教科名

maths（数学）＊アメリカ英語では math
science（理科）＊ scientist は「科学者」
English（英語）＊ England の接尾辞が -ish になったもの
history（歴史）＊ historical（歴史の）と historic（歴史的な）を混同しないよう注意
physics（物理）＊ physic はもともとは「物質の」を意味する形容詞
biology（生物学）＊ bio の語源は「生きる」、logy は「学問」
chemistry（化学）＊ chemist は「化学者」
linguistics（言語学）＊ ling の語源は「舌」、linguist は「言語学者」

▶ 解 説

指示文のパラフレーズ

▶ The table indicates the differences in the number of <u>maths, science, English and history classes</u> that 15-year-old students take every week at school <mark>in four East Asian countries</mark>.

下線部のように、指示文と異なる言い回しになるようにパラフレーズすることが重要です。教科名は具体的に挙げていますが、国名についてはすべて述べるのではなく、ハイライト部分では「4つの東アジアの国」という表現に変えています。

全体の描写

▶ While the amount of time that some subjects are studied differs greatly, others show less of a difference.

表に示された詳細な情報は組み込まずに、全体から読み取れる概要的な内容を描写しています。ここでは、各国で各教科を何時間学んでいるのかという具体的な数値には触れずに、「学ぶ時間に大きな違いがある教科もあれば、そうでない教科もある」とまとめています。

この単語、たいせつ！

☐ indicate
　⑩示す

このフレーズ、たいせつ！

☐ amount of time
　時間数

☐ show less of a difference
　そこまでの違いが見られない

Body 1

4 The table below indicates the number of times that 15-year-old school students in China, Korea, Japan, and Taiwan study four different subjects per week. Summarise the information by selecting and reporting the main features, and make comparisons where relevant.

訳 下の表は、中国、韓国、日本、台湾の15歳の生徒が、4種類の教科を1週間に学ぶ時間数を示している。主な特徴を選んで伝え、必要に応じて比較をしながら、情報をまとめなさい。

	Maths	Science	English	History
China	6	3	10	4
Korea	5	6	12	2
Japan	8	5	7	3
Taiwan	5	6	10	3

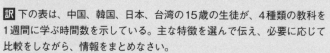

Q モデルエッセーより ||||||||||||||||||||||||||||||||||||||||||||||||||||||||||||||||||||||||| |||||||||||||||

Schools invest the most time in teaching students English in all of the four countries except Japan. Korea takes the lead at 12 hours per week, while China and Taiwan tie in second place. However, in Japan, students only study English for seven classes every week, which is only a little more than half the time that Korean students spend. On the other hand, Japanese students spend eight classes learning maths, which is more than in any other country. Korea and Taiwan do not seem to be as enthusiastic about this subject since they only require students to study it for five classes.

訳 日本以外のすべての国において、学校は生徒に英語を教えるために最も多くの時間を割いている。韓国が1週間に12時間で先頭を行っている。そして、中国と台湾が2位で並んでいる。しかし日本では、生徒は1週間に7時間しか英語を学んでおらず、これは韓国の生徒の半分より少し多い程度でしかない。その一方で、日本人は他のどの国よりも多い8時間を、数学を学ぶことに使っている。韓国や台湾は5時間しかこの教科を学ぶことを義務づけていないことからすると、この教科に対してそれほど熱心ではなさそうである。

▶ 解 説

差が比較的大きい教科

▶ Schools invest the most time in teaching students English in all of the four countries except Japan. Korea takes the lead at 12 hours per week, while China and Taiwan tie in second place. However, in Japan, students only study English for seven classes every week, which is only a little more than half the time that Korean students spend. On the other hand, Japanese students spend eight classes learning maths, which is more than in any other country. Korea and Taiwan do not seem to be as enthusiastic about this subject since they only require students to study it for five classes.

　ここでは、表の最高値と最低値を比較して、比較的数値の違いが大きい英語と数学について記しています。ハイライト部分のように関係代名詞の非制限用法を用いて、単に日本の生徒が週に何時間英語を学んでいるのかという数値を示すのではなく、他の要素との比較によって時間数の少なさを強調するのも良いでしょう。

この単語、たいせつ！

☐ invest
　動投資する
☐ except
　前〜以外
☐ tie
　動同点になる
☐ enthusiastic
　形熱心な
☐ require
　動要求する

このフレーズ、たいせつ！

☐ take the lead
　先頭を行く
☐ on the other hand
　一方で

Body 2

4 The table below indicates the number of times that 15-year-old school students in China, Korea, Japan, and Taiwan study four different subjects per week. Summarise the information by selecting and reporting the main features, and make comparisons where relevant.

訳 下の表は、中国、韓国、日本、台湾の15歳の生徒が、4種類の教科を1週間に学ぶ時間数を示している。主な特徴を選んで伝え、必要に応じて比較をしながら、情報をまとめなさい。

	Maths	Science	English	History
China	6	3	10	4
Korea	5	6	12	2
Japan	8	5	7	3
Taiwan	5	6	10	3

 モデルエッセーより ||||||||||||||||||||||||||||||||||||||||||||||||||||||||||||||||||||||||||||||

There is only a slight difference in the amount of time used for studying science. The top countries are Korea and Taiwan at six classes per week, whereas the lowest is China at three classes. The subject which is most equally emphasised in all four countries is history, since each dedicates two to four classes every week to this subject.

訳 理科を学ぶために使われた時間には、わずかな差しか見られなかった。(授業時間数が)最多の国は週に6時間の韓国と台湾であり、最少なのは3時間の中国である。どの国も毎週2〜4時間を費やしていることから、4つの国すべてにおいて最も均等に重要視されている教科は歴史である。

！ コロケーション

コロケーションとは相性が良い単語同士の結びつきを指し、アカデミックライティングの「型」を成す大切な要素です。コロケーションを調べるには、ウェブ上の Oxford Collocation Dictionary がおすすめです。例えば difference を入力すると、以下のような、使用頻度が高く相性が良い形容詞をリストの形で確認することができます。

slight difference(わずかな違い)　　　　substantial difference(かなりの違い)
significant difference(重大な違い)　　　fundamental difference(根本的な違い)
noticeable difference(顕著な違い)

解 説

差が比較的小さい教科

▶ There is only a slight difference in the amount of time used for studying science. The top countries are Korea and Taiwan at six classes per week, whereas the lowest is China at three classes. The subject which is most equally emphasised in all four countries is history, since each dedicates two to four classes every week to this subject.

本論2（Body 2）では、比較的時間の差が小さい理科と歴史について描写しています。最初に、理科の授業時間数にあまり大きな差がないことを述べています。そして、それを数値で示すために、最も授業時間数が多い韓国と台湾の数値を挙げています。そして最も授業時間数が少ない中国の数値についても、接続詞のwhereas（一方で）を用いて言及しています。次に、最も授業時間数に差が見られなかった歴史について、各国で毎週何時間くらい歴史を学んでいるのかを具体的に述べています。このように、主張の後に根拠を続けることで一貫性が保たれます。

📖 表の問題で使えるコロケーション

☐the lowest percentage
最も低い割合
☐double the price of A
Aの価格の2倍
☐estimated figures
推定された数字
☐the largest difference
最も大きな違い
☐at first glance
一見すると
☐as an overall trend
全体の傾向として
☐as shown in the table
表から分かる通り
☐as can be seen
見て分かる通り
☐as it is presented
示されているように
☐to some extent
ある程度

Task 1

5 地図の問題 Map

The maps below are of a certain town in 1995 and in the present day. Summarise the information by selecting and reporting the main features, and make comparisons where relevant.

1995

Present

Brainstorming

Introduction ▶ 指示文のパラフレーズと全体の描写をする
- *changes a town has gone through*
- *the town has changed greatly over the past years*

Body 1 ▶ 北部の変化

Changes in the northern part
- *fishing port is gone* •*market→hotels*
- *shopping district was built*

Body 2 ▶ 南部の変化

Changes in the southern part
- *park→golf course* •*more houses and new apartments*
- *farmland on west side of river→park* •*a school was built*

Conclusion ▶ 上記を踏まえ全体をまとめる
- *town has changed to accommodate more people living in and visiting the town*
- *lots of development*

Model Essay

Introduction

The two parallel maps show the major changes that a certain town has gone through between 1995 and the present. A previously small, suburban seaside town has now flourished and been redeveloped into a thriving urban centre.

Body 1

In the northern part of the town, around the coastal area, the market has been replaced with several hotels. The old fishing port where boats were previously docked no longer exists, and a brand-new shopping district has been built on the western part of the shore, within easy access for any hotel guests.

Body 2

Further south, the central area, which used to be a park, is now a golf course. It can be seen that the amount of residential housing has increased, including some new apartments built along a newly created road. The west side of the river used to be sprawling farmland, but it has now been transformed into a park and a school.

Conclusion

There are significant signs that the layout of the town has been deliberately altered from a more isolated small community to a much bigger, diverse utilisation of space. This town has developed in many ways to accommodate and entertain the increasing numbers of people that are coming to live in or visit the area.

(205 words)

Introduction

5 The maps below are of a certain town in 1995 and in the present day. Summarise the information by selecting and reporting the main features, and make comparisons where relevant.

訳 下の地図は、ある町の1995年と現在を示したものである。主な特徴を選んで伝え、必要に応じて比較をしながら、情報をまとめなさい。

O_{モデルエッセーより} ||||||||||||||||||||||||||||||||||||||||||||||||||||||||||||||||||||||||||| ||||||||||

The two parallel maps show the major changes that a certain town has gone through between 1995 and the present. A previously small, suburban seaside town has now flourished and been redeveloped into a thriving urban centre.

訳 2つの並んだ地図は、ある町が1995年から現在までの間に経験した大きな変化を示している。以前は小さな郊外の海辺の町だったのが、今では発展を遂げ、繁栄する都心へと再開発されている。

! **地図の問題で使える動詞**

make
Drivers need to make a left at the second set of traffic lights.
（ドライバーは2つ目の信号を左折する必要がある）

include
Attractions in the zoo include a penguin enclosure and a pig pen.
（動物園内のアトラクションには、ペンギンの飼育場や豚舎などがある）

happen
Construction is happening in the old quarter. （旧市街地では工事が行われている）

take place
Community events take place in the town hall. （地域のイベントはタウンホールで行われる）

▶ 解説

指示文のパラフレーズ

▶ The two parallel maps show the major changes that a certain town has gone through between 1995 and the present.

　地図の問題では、まれに1つの地図のみが出題されることもありますが、通常は、過去と現在や過去と未来の地図を比較して描写するスキルが求められます。今回は、ある地域の過去と現在を比べて変化を描写するタスクです。まず指示文のin 1995 and in the present day を between 1995 and the present に言い換え、major change（大きな変化）があったことを述べています。その際に、「困難などを（乗り越える）経験をする」という意味を持つgo through を用いているのもポイントです。

全体の描写

▶ A previously small, suburban seaside town has now flourished and been redeveloped into a thriving urban centre.

　ここでは細かい変化については触れず、以前は小さかった町が今では繁栄する都心になっていることを、現在完了形を用いて表現しています。

変化の表現　右側に＊で名詞を示しています。

replace（置き換える）　　　＊ replacement（置き換え）
convert（変換する）　　　　＊ conversion（変換）
renovate（改修する）　　　＊ renovation（改修）
transform（変形する）　　　＊ transformation（変形）
alter（部分的に変える）　　＊ alteration（変更）
modernise（現代化する）　＊ modernisation（現代化）
urbanise（都市化する）　　＊ urbanisation（都市化）
revolutionise（改革する）　＊ revolution（改革）
industrialise（産業化する）＊ industrialisation（産業化）
merge（併合する）　　　　　＊ merger（併合）

Body 1

5 The maps below are of a certain town in 1995 and in the present day. Summarise the information by selecting and reporting the main features, and make comparisons where relevant.

訳 下の地図は、ある町の1995年と現在を示したものである。主な特徴を選んで伝え、必要に応じて比較をしながら、情報をまとめなさい。

1995

Present

◯ モデルエッセーより ||||||||||||||||||||||||||||||||||||||||||||||||||||||||||||||||||||||||||||||

In the northern part of the town, around the coastal area, the market has been replaced with several hotels. The old fishing port where boats were previously docked no longer exists, and a brand-new shopping district has been built on the western part of the shore, within easy access for any hotel guests.

訳 町の北部、沿岸エリアでは、市場に代わっていくつかのホテルができた。以前は船が停泊していた古い漁港はもはやなくなり、海岸の西側部分に新しいショッピング街が建設され、あらゆるホテルの宿泊客が簡単にアクセスできるようになった。

💬 方位の表現

地図の問題では north（北）east（東）west（西）south（南）といった方位・方角を表現する必要があります。以下のような頻出表現とともに覚えておきましょう。

in the west of A（A の西側に）
There is a fountain in the west of the city.（街の西側には噴水がある）
in the north-east of A（A の北東に）
The library is in the north-east of the town.（図書館は町の北東にある）
slightly to the east of A（A のやや東側に）
The parking area was relocated slightly to the east of the map.（駐車場は地図のやや東側に移設された）
from west to east（西から東に）
There is a line of small shops from west to east.（西から東に小さな店が並んでいる）

解 説

町の北部の変化

▶ In the northern part of the town, around the coastal area, the market has been replaced with several hotels. The old fishing port where boats were previously docked no longer exists, and a brand-new shopping district has been built on the western part of the shore, within easy access for any hotel guests.

本論1（Body 1）では、町の北部である沿岸エリアの変化について書いています。1文目では現在完了形の受動態を用いて、市場が複数のホテルに取って代わられたことを描写しています。2文目では、2つの地図を比べてなくなったものと追加されたものを詳細に描写しています。地図の問題に関し、どのように情報を整理して描写するかの決まりはありません。この例のようにエリアごとで分けたり、変化が大きいところと少ないところに分けたりして説明すると良いでしょう。

 no longer

no longer は「もはや～ない」という意味で、これまであった存在がなくなったときなどに使うことができます。同様の意味の not any longer は口語表現なので注意しましょう。Some people think that newspapers are no longer necessary. To what extent do you agree or disagree?（新聞はもはや必要ないと考える人もいる。あなたは［これに］どの程度、賛成あるいは反対しますか？）といった指示文が、過去の IELTS のライティング Task 2 に登場しています。

この単語、たいせつ！

☐ replace
　働 置き換える
☐ dock
　働 停留させる
☐ exist
　働 存在する
☐ brand-new
　形 新しい

このフレーズ、たいせつ！

☐ coastal area
　海岸沿いのエリア
☐ shopping district
　ショッピング街

Body 2

5 The maps below are of a certain town in 1995 and in the present day. Summarise the information by selecting and reporting the main features, and make comparisons where relevant.

訳 下の地図は、ある町の1995年と現在を示したものである。主な特徴を選んで伝え、必要に応じて比較をしながら、情報をまとめなさい。

1995

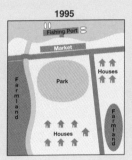

Present

🔍 モデルエッセーより ||||||||||||||||||||||||||||||||||||||||||||||||||||||||||||||||||||||||||||||

Further south, the central area, which used to be a park, is now a golf course. It can be seen that the amount of residential housing has increased, including some new apartments built along a newly created road. The west side of the river used to be sprawling farmland, but it has now been transformed into a park and a school.

訳 南へ行くと、かつて公園だった中心部は今、ゴルフコースになっている。新たにできた道沿いに建てられた新しいアパートなど、住宅が増えたことが見て取れる。川の西側にはかつて農地が広がっていたが、今では公園と学校に変わっている。

建物に関する表現　　右側に＊で名詞を示しています。

add（加える）	＊ addition（追加）
erect（立てる）	＊ erection（建設）
plant（植える）	＊ plantation（植え込み）
establish（設立する）	＊ establishment（設立）
relocate（再移動する）	＊ relocation（再移動）
install（取りつける）	＊ installment（取りつけ）
construct（建設する）	＊ construction（建設）
reconstruct（再建設する）	＊ reconstruction（再建設）

解 説

町の南部の変化

▶ Further south, the central area, which used to be a park, is now a golf course. It can be seen that the amount of residential housing has increased, including some new apartments built along a newly created road. The west side of the river used to be sprawling farmland, but it has now been transformed into a park and a school.

　本論2（Body 2）では、町の南部の変化について描写しています。ここでも本論1（Body 1）と同じように、ある過去の時点から現在までの様子を表現する現在完了形を主に用いて伝えています。used to be（かつて～であった）は、過去に何であったかを描写する表現で、地図の問題では必須のフレーズです。

「拡大」に関する表現

　地図の問題では変化を表現することが求められます。適切な単語を用いてオリジナルの「型」を作り、どのような変化も表現できるようにしておきましょう。ここでは「拡大」の表現を紹介します。右側に＊で示した名詞も一緒に覚えて、より高得点を狙いましょう。

enlarge（拡大する）　＊ enlargement（拡大）
It costs an extra 50 pence to enlarge as well as photocopy.
（コピーだけでなく拡大にも、50ペンスが追加でかかる）
extend（拡張する）　＊ extension（拡張）
The school field extends to the edge of the forest.
（学校のグラウンドは森の端まで広がっている）
expand（拡大する）　＊ expansion（拡大）
The nearby park has been expanded to include a dog park.
（近くの公園が大きくなり、ドッグパークができた）
elongate（延長する）　＊ elongation（延長）
The shape elongates and then solidifies.（形状が伸びて固まる）
redevelop（再開発させる）　＊ redevelopment（再開発）
The council advised us to redevelop the whole system.
（協議会は私たちに、システム全体の再開発を勧めた）

Conclusion

5 The maps below are of a certain town in 1995 and in the present day. Summarise the information by selecting and reporting the main features, and make comparisons where relevant.

訳 下の地図は、ある町の1995年と現在を示したものである。主な特徴を選んで伝え、必要に応じて比較をしながら、情報をまとめなさい。

🔍 **モデルエッセーより** |||||||||||||||||||||||||||||||||||||||||||||||||||||||||||||||||||||||| |||||||||||

There are significant signs that the layout of the town has been deliberately altered from a more isolated small community to a much bigger, diverse utilisation of space. This town has developed in many ways to accommodate and entertain the increasing numbers of people that are coming to live in or visit the area.

訳 町のレイアウトが、より孤立した小さなコミュニティから、はるかに大きく多様な空間の活用へと意図的に変更されたことが顕著に示されている。この町は、この地域に居住あるいは訪問目的でやってくる、ますます増え続ける人々を受け入れ楽しませるために、さまざまな方法で発展してきた。

💬 **develop の意味と使い方**

develop には自動詞の「発展する」という意味と、他動詞の「発展させる」という意味があります。例えば、Japan developed. は過去に日本が自らの力で発展したことを意味し、Japan was developed. は過去に何かによって発展させられたと解釈できます。現在完了形を使った Japan has developed. は、過去のある時点から今までにかけて発展してきたことを意味し、Japan has been developed. は、過去のある時点から今までにかけて何かの影響を受けて発展させられたと解釈できます。また、現在完了進行形の Japan has been developing. は、過去のある時点から今もなお、発展し続けていることを意味します。developing country（発展し続けている国：発展途上国）、developed country（発展させられた国：先進国）の違いにも注意しましょう。

解 説

全体の描写

▶ There are significant signs that the layout of the town has been deliberately altered from a more isolated small community to a much bigger, diverse utilisation of space. This town has developed in many ways to accommodate and entertain the increasing numbers of people that are coming to live in or visit the area.

　ここでは地図上の変化を、高度な表現を用いて少し発展的にまとめています。後半部分では、地図に見られる変化を基に、より多くの人が住み、訪れられるように町が発展してきたことを述べています。客観性を常に意識して、主観的な分析や根拠のない解釈を書いてしまわないように気をつけましょう。

この単語、たいせつ!

- [ ] deliberately
  圖意図的に
- [ ] isolated
  圈孤立した
- [ ] accommodate
  動生活・滞在のための場所を提供する
- [ ] entertain
  動楽しませる

このフレーズ、たいせつ!

- [ ] diverse utilisation of space
  多様な空間の活用

地図の問題で使えるコロケーション

- [ ] residential housing
  住宅
- [ ] central area
  中心のエリア
- [ ] coastal area
  海岸沿いのエリア
- [ ] pedestrian area
  歩行者エリア
- [ ] brand-new facilities
  真新しい施設
- [ ] a newly created road
  新しく造られた道路
- [ ] located in the north
  北側に位置している
- [ ] situated in the centre
  中央に位置している
- [ ] in the vicinity of A
  Aの近くに
- [ ] from north to south
  北から南に

Task 1

6 ダイアグラムの問題　Diagram

The following diagram shows how crayons are made. Summarise the information by selecting and reporting the main features.

1 Wax is melted

2 Chemicals are added to improve quality

3 Colouring is added

4 Mixture is blended for one hour

5 Mixture is moulded into crayon shapes

6 Moulds are put in water to harden mixture

7 Crayons are labelled on a rotating machine
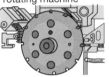

8 Crayons are sorted by colour
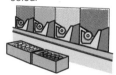

9 Crayons are packed in boxes
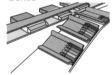

10 Contents of boxes are checked manually

˗Brainstorming

| Introduction | 指示文のパラフレーズと全体の描写をする |

- *industrial process of manufacturing crayons*

| Body 1 | 前半の製造工程を描写する |

- *steps 1-6*

| Body 2 | 後半の製造工程を描写する |

- *steps 7-10*

Model Essay

Introduction

This diagram explains the steps involved in the industrial process of manufacturing crayons. There are 10 stages in the entire process, starting first with melting the wax and ending in the finished crayon boxes being checked manually.

Body 1

First of all, the main ingredient, wax, is melted at a high temperature. Right after this, a blend of chemicals is added to improve the quality of the crayons. Then, colouring is added and the mixture is blended thoroughly for one hour. After this, the mixture is poured into a mould to shape the crayons and the wax is hardened by putting the mould into cold water.

Body 2

The hardened crayons are then taken out of the mould and labelled one by one on a rotating machine. Following this step, the labelled crayons are sorted by colour and packed into boxes. Finally, the contents of the boxes are checked by hand to ensure the quality of the final product.

(155 words)

Introduction

6 The following diagram shows how crayons are made. Summarise the information by selecting and reporting the main features.

訳 次のダイアグラム（略図）はクレヨンの製造方法を示している。主な特徴を選んで伝え、情報をまとめなさい。

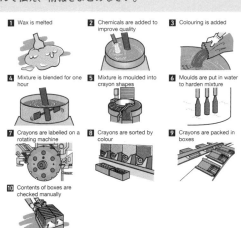

1 Wax is melted
2 Chemicals are added to improve quality
3 Colouring is added
4 Mixture is blended for one hour
5 Mixture is moulded into crayon shapes
6 Moulds are put in water to harden mixture
7 Crayons are labelled on a rotating machine
8 Crayons are sorted by colour
9 Crayons are packed in boxes
10 Contents of boxes are checked manually

 モデルエッセーより ||||||||||||||||||||||||||||||||||||||||||||||||||||||||||||||||||||||||||||| |||||||||||

This diagram explains the steps involved in the industrial process of manufacturing crayons. There are 10 stages in the entire process, starting first with melting the wax and ending in the finished crayon boxes being checked manually.

訳 この図はクレヨンの製造工程に伴う段階を説明している。工程全体には、10の段階がある。最初はワックスを溶かすことから始まり、完成したクレヨンの箱を手作業で確認して終わる。

⚠ ダイアグラムの問題

ダイアグラムの問題は、ライティングの中で対策が最も難しいタイプの問題です。製造手順や説明書、輸送のロジスティクスなどが出題されます。主に「自然のプロセス」と「人工のプロセス」の 2 種類があり、「自然のプロセス」のダイアグラムは、人間、動植物、水の循環、牛のミルクなど、さまざまな自然界のプロセスや仕組みを説明したものです。「人工のプロセス」のダイアグラムは、ビール、コーヒー、チョコレート、セメント、レンガなどの製品が作られるプロセスについてのものです。

▶ 解 説

指示文のパラフレーズ

▶ This diagram explains the steps involved in the industrial process of manufacturing crayons.

　ダイアグラムの問題の導入（Introduction）も、他の問題と同様に指示文のパラフレーズから始めます。ここではstep（段階）を用いましたが、同様の意味のstageも使えます。また、生命などの循環はcycle、動植物などの進化はdevelopment、製造過程はproductionなどで表せます。描写する対象に合わせて適切な語を用いましょう。

全体の描写

▶ There are 10 stages in the entire process, starting first with melting the wax and ending in the finished crayon boxes being checked manually.

　次に「全部で何段階あるのか」や「最初と最後の段階に何が行われるか」を簡潔に描写します。図に記載された表現を適宜パラフレーズして説明しましょう。

📖 ダイアグラムに関して使えるコロケーション

☐ life cycle
　生命循環

☐ entire process
　全体の過程

☐ cyclical process
　循環過程

☐ man-made materials
　人工の素材

☐ halfway through
　〜の途中で

☐ production stage
　生産段階

☐ operation phase
　運用フェーズ

☐ deliver new products
　新製品を配達する

☐ sent to the factory
　工場に送られる

☐ following this procedure
　この手順に従って

☐ in a logical sequence
　論理的な順序で

この**単語**、たいせつ！

☐ industrial
　⑱産業の

☐ melt
　⑲溶かす

☐ manually
　⑳手で

この**フレーズ**、たいせつ！

☐ end in A
　Aに終わる

113

Body 1

6 The following diagram shows how crayons are made. Summarise the information by selecting and reporting the main features.

訳 次のダイアグラム（略図）はクレヨンの製造方法を示している。主な特徴を選んで伝え、情報をまとめなさい。

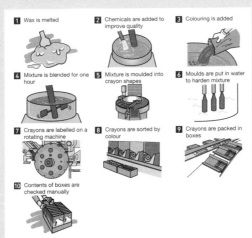

1 Wax is melted

2 Chemicals are added to improve quality

3 Colouring is added

4 Mixture is blended for one hour

5 Mixture is moulded into crayon shapes

6 Moulds are put in water to harden mixture

7 Crayons are labelled on a rotating machine

8 Crayons are sorted by colour

9 Crayons are packed in boxes

10 Contents of boxes are checked manually

○ モデルエッセーより ||||||||||||||||||||||||||||||||||||||||||||||||||||||||||||||||| ||||||||||||

First of all, the main ingredient, wax, is melted at a high temperature. Right after this, a blend of chemicals is added to improve the quality of the crayons. Then, colouring is added and the mixture is blended thoroughly for one hour. After this, the mixture is poured into a mould to shape the crayons and the wax is hardened by putting the mould into cold water.

訳 最初に主原料であるワックスが高温で溶かされる。その直後に、クレヨンの品質を向上させるために化学物質が加えられる。それから顔料が加えられ、その混合体は1時間しっかりとかき混ぜられる。その後、その混合体はクレヨンの形にするために型に流し込まれ、型を冷水につけることによってワックスが固められる。

解 説

前半の製造工程について

▶ First of all, the main ingredient, wax, is melted at a high temperature. Right after this, a blend of chemicals is added to improve the quality of the crayons. Then, colouring is added and the mixture is blended thoroughly for one hour. After this, the mixture is poured into a mould to shape the crayons and the wax is hardened by putting the mould into cold water.

ダイアグラムの問題は最も難易度が高く、「型」が通用しないことがあります。図やプロセスを見ながら客観的に描写していくスキルが求められます。本論1（Body 1）で、前半部分である1〜6の製造工程を描写し、残りを本論2（Body 2）で描写しています。下線部のような順序の表現を巧みに使いましょう。

 順序のディスコースマーカー

ダイアグラムの問題では、以下のような表現を用いて各プロセスを詳細に描写していきましょう。

・最初に
First ...（最初に ...）
To begin with ...（最初に ...）
The first step is ...（最初のステップは ...）
In the first stage ...（最初のステージでは ...）
The process begins with ...（プロセスは ... から始まる）
・次に
Next ...（次に ...）
Afterwards ...（その後 ...）
Subsequently ...（その後 ...）
Following this step ...（このステップに続いて ...）
Once A is done ...（A が終わったら ...）
・最後に
Finally ...（ついに ...）
Lastly ...（最後に ...）
Eventually ...（結局は ...）
At the final stage ...（最後のステージで ...）

Body 2

6 The following diagram shows how crayons are made.
Summarise the information by selecting and reporting the main features.

訳 次のダイアグラム（略図）はクレヨンの製造方法を示している。主な特徴を選んで伝え、情報をまとめなさい。

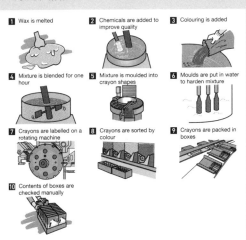

1 Wax is melted

2 Chemicals are added to improve quality

3 Colouring is added

4 Mixture is blended for one hour

5 Mixture is moulded into crayon shapes

6 Moulds are put in water to harden mixture

7 Crayons are labelled on a rotating machine

8 Crayons are sorted by colour

9 Crayons are packed in boxes

10 Contents of boxes are checked manually

○ モデルエッセーより ‖‖‖

The hardened crayons are then taken out of the mould and labelled one by one on a rotating machine. Following this step, the labelled crayons are sorted by colour and packed into boxes. Finally, the contents of the boxes are checked by hand to ensure the quality of the final product.

訳 固められたクレヨンはその後、型から取り出され、回転する機械の上で個々にラベルづけされる。この段階に続いて、ラベルづけされたクレヨンは色ごとに分けられ、箱に詰められる。最後に、完成した製品の質を保証するために、箱の中身が手作業で確認される。

▶ 解 説

後半の製造工程について

▶ The hardened crayons are <u>then</u> taken out of the mould and labelled one by one on a rotating machine. <u>Following this step</u>, the labelled crayons are sorted by colour and packed into boxes. <u>Finally</u>, the contents of the boxes are checked by hand to ensure the quality of the final product.

　本論2（Body 2）で後半部分の製造工程を描写し、締めくくっています。本論1（Body 1）と同様に、下線部のような順序の表現を活用しましょう。スペリングはイギリス英語かアメリカ英語で統一し、混在させないようにしましょう。

この単語、たいせつ！

☐ label
　動 ラベルづけする
☐ sort
　動 分類する

このフレーズ、たいせつ！

☐ rotating machine
　回転する機械
☐ ensure the quality
　質を保証する

 イギリス英語とアメリカ英語

イギリス英語とアメリカ英語を混在させると減点対象となりますので、一貫性を保つことが重要です。日本人学習者が間違えやすい単語の例を紹介します。

イギリス英語	アメリカ英語	日本語	イギリス英語	アメリカ英語	日本語
mould	mold	型	enrol	enroll	入会する
colour	color	色	enquiry	inquiry	問い合わせ
favourite	favorite	お気に入りの	jewellery	jewelry	宝石
rumour	rumor	うわさ	organise	organize	組織する
endeavour	endeavor	努力	recognise	recognize	認識する
honour	honor	誇り	memorise	memorize	記憶する
centre	center	中心	destabilise	destabilize	不安定にする
theatre	theater	劇場	encyclopaedia	encyclopedia	百科事典

Task 1

7 2つのグラフを組み合わせた問題 Combination 1

The bar graph below shows the average amount of overtime hours per month for people of five different professions. The pie chart illustrates the occupations of those who suffer from mental illness. Summarise the information, and make comparisons where relevant.

Average Overtime Hours per Month

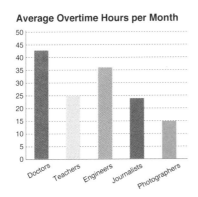

Occupations of People with Mental Illnesses

-Brainstorming

Introduction ▶ 指示文のパラフレーズと全体の描写をする
- correlation between individuals' professions and having a mental illness
- the more overtime hours, the more people suffer from mental illness

Body 1 ▶ 棒グラフについて
About the Bar Graph
- doctors work the most overtime hours: about 43
- engineers are next: a little over 35
- teachers and journalists: around 25
- photographers: about one third of doctors

Body 2 ▶ 円グラフについて
About the Pie Chart
- the more overtime, the higher the risk of mental illness is
- doctors are number one: 33%   • engineers: 28%
- teachers and journalists: around 15%   • photographers are last

Conclusion ▶ 上記を踏まえ全体をまとめる
- risk of mental illness gets higher the more you work

118

Model Essay

Introduction

The two graphs indicate a correlation between individuals' professions and the likelihood of having a mental illness. It can be said that the more time one is required to work outside of regular hours, the higher the risk of falling into mental illness becomes.

Body 1

Doctors work the most extra time, spending around 43 hours working overtime. The next most demanding job is engineers, since they put in an average of a little over 35 hours monthly doing extra work. At about 25 hours each month, teachers and journalists come in next, and photographers only spend about one third of the time that doctors do overworking.

Body 2

When combining the data from both the bar graph and the pie chart, it is made clear that the number of people who have mental illnesses rises in proportion to how much time they work. Doctors account for 33% of all mental illness patients, and engineers follow closely behind at 28%. Teachers and journalists make up around a total of 30%, and photographers have the lowest percentage.

Conclusion

Overall, the amount of overtime differs greatly depending on each job, and the more overtime hours one has, the more likely one is to suffer from mental issues.

(200 words)

Introduction

7 The bar graph below shows the average amount of overtime hours per month for people of five different professions. The pie chart illustrates the occupations of those who suffer from mental illness. Summarise the information, and make comparisons where relevant.

訳 下の棒グラフは、5種類の職業従事者たちの月間平均残業時間数を示している。円グラフは、精神病を患う人々の職業を明らかにしている。情報をまとめ、必要に応じて比較しなさい。

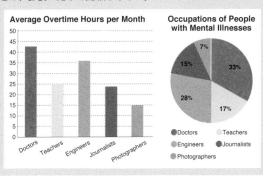

Average Overtime Hours per Month

Doctors, Teachers, Engineers, Journalists, Photographers

Occupations of People with Mental Illnesses

- Doctors 33%
- Teachers 7%
- Engineers 28%
- Journalists 17%
- Photographers 15%

モデルエッセーより ||||||||||||||||||||||||||||||||||||||||||||||||||||||||||||||||||||||||| ||||||||||||

The two graphs indicate a correlation between individuals' professions and the likelihood of having a mental illness. It can be said that the more time one is required to work outside of regular hours, the higher the risk of falling into mental illness becomes.

訳 この2つのグラフは、個人の職業と精神疾患の可能性との相関を示している。正規時間外で働かなければならない時間が多ければ多いほど、精神病になるリスクが高まると言える。

解 説

指示文のパラフレーズ

▶ The two graphs indicate a correlation between individuals' professions and the likelihood of having a mental illness.

　棒グラフと円グラフを組み合わせた問題で、両方のグラフを読み取り描写するスキルが求められます。ここでは、長めの指示文を 1 文にまとめて簡潔にパラフレーズしています。

全体の描写

▶ It can be said that the more time one is required to work outside of regular hours, the higher the risk of falling into mental illness becomes.

　各グラフに示された詳細な情報は組み込まずに、概要的な内容を描写しています。ここでは「残業時間が長いほど、精神病になるリスクが高くなる」ということを客観的に述べています。

この単語、たいせつ！

☐ correlation
　㊅ 相関
☐ likelihood
　㊅ 可能性
☐ risk
　㊅ 危険性

このフレーズ、たいせつ！

☐ outside of regular hours
　正規の時間外で
☐ fall into mental illness
　精神病に陥る

 「～する人」「～な人」の表し方

「～する人」を表す際、関係代名詞の who を用いて後置修飾の形にすると冗長になってしまいます。例えば、people who have teaching experience は、前置詞の with を用いることで people with teaching experience（指導経験がある人）と、より簡潔な表現にできます。また「人」を表す接尾辞の -er の入った teacher（先生）、driver（運転手）、speaker（話者）や、より専門性の高い人を指す接尾辞 -or の入った、actor（俳優）や professor（教授）なども使えます。他にも the ＋形容詞で「～な人」を表すことができ、the poor は「貧乏な人」となります。さらに、significant other や loved one は「大切な人」を意味するので覚えておきましょう。

121

Body 1

7 The bar graph below shows the average amount of overtime hours per month for people of five different professions. The pie chart illustrates the occupations of those who suffer from mental illness. Summarise the information, and make comparisons where relevant.

訳 下の棒グラフは、5種類の職業従事者たちの月間平均残業時間数を示している。円グラフは、精神病を患う人々の職業を明らかにしている。情報をまとめ、必要に応じて比較しなさい。

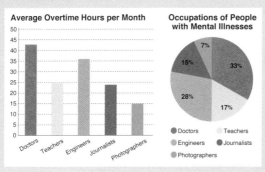

Q モデルエッセーより |||||||||||||||||||||||||||||||||||||||||||||||||||||||||||||||||||||||||||||||||||| |||||||||||

Doctors work the most extra time, spending around 43 hours working overtime. The next most demanding job is engineers, since they put in an average of a little over 35 hours monthly doing extra work. At about 25 hours each month, teachers and journalists come in next, and photographers only spend about one third of the time that doctors do overworking.

訳 医師が最も残業が多く、約43時間残業をしている。次にきつい仕事は、月に平均35時間ちょっとを残業に費やしているエンジニアである。その次が毎月約25時間の教師とジャーナリストであり、写真家は医師の3分の1の時間しか残業をしていない。

解 説

棒グラフについて

▶ Doctors work the most extra time, spending
  <u>around 43 hours</u> working overtime. The next most
  demanding job is engineers, since they put in an
  average of a little <u>over 35 hours</u> monthly doing extra
  work. At <u>about 25 hours</u> each month, teachers and
  journalists come in next, and photographers only
  spend about one third of the time that doctors do
  overworking.

　5つの職業すべての順位と残業時間を、下線部のように
具体的な数値を挙げて示しています。基本的には、時間
数が多い職業から描写していくと分かりやすくなります。

 ## 職業の表現

IELTS では職業に関する表現が頻出です。単に職業名を覚えるだけでなく、英英辞典の定義も併せ
て単語を覚えていきましょう。以下は Cambridge Dictionary における職業を表す単語の定義です。
さまざまな職業について英語で説明できるようにしておきましょう。

librarian（司書）：a person who works in a library
astronomer（天文学者）：someone who studies astronomy
dentist（歯科医）：a person whose job is treating people's teeth
gardener（庭師）：someone who works in a garden, growing and taking care of plants
mechanic（機械工）：someone whose job is repairing the engines of vehicles and other
　　　　　　　　　　　　machines
pharmacist（薬剤師）：a person who is trained to prepare and give out medicines in a
　　　　　　　　　　　　hospital or shop
secretary（秘書）：someone who works in an office, writing letters, making phone calls,
　　　　　　　　　　　and arranging meetings for a person or for an organization
translator（翻訳家）：a person whose job is changing words, especially written words, into
　　　　　　　　　　　a different language
accountant（会計士）：someone who keeps or examines the records of money received,
　　　　　　　　　　　paid, and owed by a company or person
architect（建築家）：a person whose job is to design new buildings and make certain that
　　　　　　　　　　　they are built correctly
plumber（配管工）：a person whose job is to supply and connect or repair water pipes,
　　　　　　　　　　　baths, toilets, etc.
carpenter（大工）：a person whose job is making and repairing wooden objects and
　　　　　　　　　　　structures

Body 2

7 The bar graph below shows the average amount of overtime hours per month for people of five different professions. The pie chart illustrates the occupations of those who suffer from mental illness. Summarise the information, and make comparisons where relevant.

訳 下の棒グラフは、5種類の職業従事者たちの月間平均残業時間数を示している。円グラフは、精神病を患う人々の職業を明らかにしている。情報をまとめ、必要に応じて比較しなさい。

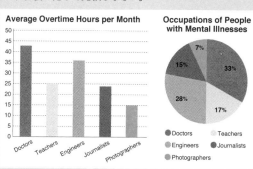

Q モデルエッセーより |||||||||||||||||||||||||||||||||||||||||||||||||||||||||||||||||||||||||||| |||||||||||

When combining the data from both the bar graph and the pie chart, it is made clear that the number of people who have mental illnesses rises, in proportion to how much time they work. Doctors account for 33% of all mental illness patients, and engineers follow closely behind at 28%. Teachers and journalists make up around a total of 30%, and photographers have the lowest percentage.

訳 棒グラフと円グラフ両方のデータを組み合わせると、精神病になる人の数は、残業時間数に比例して上昇することが明らかになる。精神病患者全体の中の33%を医師が占め、エンジニアは28%と僅差で続いている。教師とジャーナリストは、合計で約30%を成し、写真家の割合は最も低い。

▶ 解 説

円グラフについて

▶ When combining the data from both the bar graph and the pie chart, it is made clear that the number of people who have mental illnesses rises in proportion to how much time they work. Doctors account for 33% of all mental illness patients, and engineers follow closely behind at 28%. Teachers and journalists make up around a total of 30%, and photographers have the lowest percentage.

本論2（Body 2）では円グラフのデータを読み取った上で、棒グラフと円グラフの両方を組み合わせたときに分かることを客観的に描写しています。各職業の人が精神病患者のどれくらいの割合を占めているのかを示すとともに、ハイライト部分では、残業時間数と精神病患者数の相関関係についても書いています。ここでも下線部のように具体的な数値を描写しています。

この単語、たいせつ！

☐ combine
　⑩組み合わせる

このフレーズ、たいせつ！

☐ rise in proportion to A
　Aに比例して上昇する

☐ account for A
　Aを占める

☐ follow closely behind
　僅差で続く

構成の表現

Task 1 では、グラフなどがどのような構成になっているかを描写するスキルが必要です。最も基本的な表現は make up で、Writing makes up around a total of 25% of IELTS.（ライティングは IELTS 全体の 25％を構成する）のように表現できます。comprise は be comprised of の形で「～から成る、～で構成される」となり、IELTS Writing is comprised of two tasks.（IELTS ライティングは 2 つのタスクで構成されている）や Japan is comprised of 47 prefectures.（日本は 47 の都道府県で構成されている）のように使います。consist は con（ともに）＋ sist（立つ）で「支えあって成り立っている」イメージがあり、能動態で IELTS consists of 4 different skills.（IELTS は 4 つの異なるスキルから構成される）のように使います。

Conclusion

7 The bar graph below shows the average amount of overtime hours per month for people of five different professions. The pie chart illustrates the occupations of those who suffer from mental illness. Summarise the information, and make comparisons where relevant.

訳 下の棒グラフは、5種類の職業従事者たちの月間平均残業時間数を示している。円グラフは、精神病を患う人々の職業を明らかにしている。情報をまとめ、必要に応じて比較しなさい。

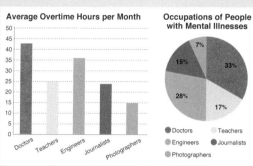

 モデルエッセーより ||||||||||||||||||||||||||||||||||||||||||||||||||||||||||||||||||||||||||||||||||||||| ||||||||||||

Overall, the amount of overtime differs greatly depending on each job, and the more overtime hours one has, the more likely one is to suffer from mental issues.

訳 概して、それぞれの職業によって残業時間は大きく異なり、残業時間が多い人ほど精神的な問題で苦しむ可能性が高い。

接頭辞 over- を含む語

over は「上に」という意味で、そこから「超過」という解釈も生まれます。接頭辞 over- で始まる単語をまとめて覚えておきましょう。

overtime（時間外労働）
overdose（過量服用）
overload（過負荷）
overflow（氾濫、過多）
overlap（重なる）
overlook（見落とす）

overrate（過大評価する）
overestimate（過大評価する）
overhaul（徹底的に見直す）
overdue（期限の過ぎた）
overspend（金を使い過ぎる）

▶ 解 説

全体の描写

▶ Overall, the amount of overtime differs greatly
depending on each job, and the more overtime
hours one has, the more likely one is to suffer from
mental issues.

ここでは、2つのグラフから読み取れる最も重要な2つ
のポイントをまとめています。まずは棒グラフだけから読
み取れる、職業による残業時間の違いについて述べ、そ
の次に、棒グラフと円グラフの両方を組み合わせたときに
明らかになる残業時間と精神病の相関関係について描写
しています。 グラフや表などを組み合わせた問題では、
それぞれから読み取れる情報を別々に書いてしまわないよ
うに気をつけましょう。

このフレーズ、たいせつ！

- [ ] depend on A
  A次第である
- [ ] suffer from
  mental issues
  精神的な問題で苦
  しむ

📖 違いや類似を表す際のコロケーション

- [ ] a dramatic difference
  劇的な違い
- [ ] a significant difference
  顕著な違い
- [ ] a subtle difference
  微妙な違い
- [ ] greatly differ from A
  Aとは大いに異なる
- [ ] gap between A and B
  AとBのギャップ
- [ ] a comparable figure
  同等の数字
- [ ] in the same way
  同様に
- [ ] a similar pattern
  同様のパターン
- [ ] apparent similarities
  明らかな類似点
- [ ] have A in common
  Aが共通している

8 案内図とグラフを組み合わせた問題 Combination 2

The maps below show the layout of a museum before and after it went through refurbishment. The pie charts underneath show the results of a questionnaire asking about the respective satisfaction levels of women, men, and children. Summarise the information by selecting and reporting the main features, and make comparisons where relevant.

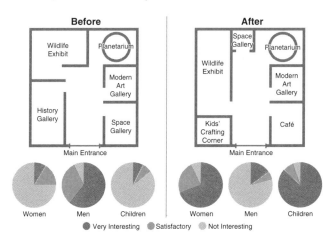

-́Brainstorming

Introduction▶ 指示文のパラフレーズと全体の描写をする
• after refurbishment, the museum had a new layout
• satisfaction levels of each customer category changed

Body 1▶ 改装前後の案内図について
• space gallery→café　• history gallery→kids' crafting corner
• made wildlife exhibit larger
• space gallery made smaller and was moved, planetarium the same

Body 2▶ 改装前後の円グラフについて
• men had high satisfaction→not so satisfied
• not so preferred by women→women liked it more
• children enjoyed museum a lot more than before

Conclusion▶ 上記を踏まえ全体をまとめる
• changes were made to the layout which changed the satisfaction levels of all customer categories

Model Essay

Introduction

A certain museum underwent refurbishment, and the maps show the respective layouts of the museum before and after renovation. The pie charts show how interesting the museum was for women, men, and children. Quite a few changes were made in the museum, and the satisfaction levels of each group changed accordingly.

Body 1

Before the refurbishment, there was a large Space Gallery close to the main entrance. However, this was changed into a café. The History Gallery, which used to be across from the Space Gallery, was also replaced by a Kids' Crafting Corner. Now, the largest section is the Wildlife Exhibit. The planetarium remained the same, but the Space Gallery was moved to be adjacent to it.

Body 2

Before renovations were carried out, about two thirds of adult male guests were highly satisfied with the content of the museum. However, now the museum is more appealing for women and children. Close to three quarters of women said that the museum was very interesting, and more than 80% of children had the same opinion.

Conclusion

Various changes were made to the museum, which resulted in a great shift in the satisfaction levels of customers.

(190 words)

Introduction

8 The maps below show the layout of a museum before and after it went through refurbishment. The pie charts underneath show the results of a questionnaire asking about the respective satisfaction levels of women, men, and children. Summarise the information by selecting and reporting the main features, and make comparisons where relevant.

訳 下の案内図は、ある博物館の改装前後のレイアウトを示している。その下の円グラフは、女性、男性、子ども、それぞれの満足度についてのアンケート結果を示している。主な特徴を選んで伝え、必要に応じて比較をしながら、情報をまとめなさい。

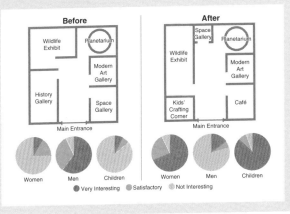

Q モデルエッセーより ||||||||||||||||||||||||||||||||||||||||||||||||||||||||||||||||||||||| ||||||||||||

A certain museum underwent refurbishment, and the maps show the respective layouts of the museum before and after renovation. The pie charts show how interesting the museum was for women, men, and children. Quite a few changes were made in the museum, and the satisfaction levels of each group changed accordingly.

訳 ある博物館で改装が行われ、案内図は改装前後の博物館のレイアウトをそれぞれ示している。円グラフはこの博物館が女性、男性、子どもにとってどれくらい興味深かったかを示している。博物館にはかなり多くの変更が加えられ、それに従って各集団の満足度も変化した。

解 説

指示文のパラフレーズ

▶ A certain museum underwent refurbishment, and the maps show the respective layouts of the museum before and after renovation. The pie charts show how interesting the museum was for women, men, and children.

案内図と円グラフが両方複数あるため、指示文のパラフレーズが長くなってしまいがちですが、できるだけ簡潔に、それぞれが何を示しているのか書きましょう。ハイライト部分が案内図、下線部が円グラフの描写です。

全体の描写

▶ Quite a few changes were made in the museum, and the satisfaction levels of each group changed accordingly.

次に、左右の案内図と円グラフから分かる変化を描写しましょう。ハイライト部分では案内図について、そして下線部では案内図の変化に応じた円グラフのデータの変化について述べています。

この単語、たいせつ！

☐ renovation
　 ⑧改装
☐ accordingly
　 ⑨それに従って

このフレーズ、たいせつ！

☐ undergo refurbishment
　 改装を行う
☐ quite a few changes
　 かなり多くの変更点
☐ satisfaction level
　 満足度

Body 1

8 The maps below show the layout of a museum before and after it went through refurbishment. The pie charts underneath show the results of a questionnaire asking about the respective satisfaction levels of women, men, and children. Summarise the information by selecting and reporting the main features, and make comparisons where relevant.

訳 下の案内図は、ある博物館の改装前後のレイアウトを示している。その下の円グラフは、女性、男性、子ども、それぞれの満足度についてのアンケート結果を示している。主な特徴を選んで伝え、必要に応じて比較をしながら、情報をまとめなさい。

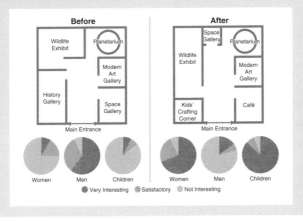

モデルエッセーより ||||||||||||||||||||||||||||||||||||||||||||||||||||||||||||||| |||||||||||

Before the refurbishment, there was a large Space Gallery close to the main entrance. However, this was changed into a café. The History Gallery, which used to be across from the Space Gallery, was also replaced by a Kids' Crafting Corner. Now, the largest section is the Wildlife Exhibit. The planetarium remained the same, but the Space Gallery was moved to be adjacent to it.

訳 改装前はメインの入り口の近くに大きな宇宙ギャラリーがあった。しかし、これはカフェに変えられた。歴史ギャラリーは宇宙ギャラリーの向かい側にあったのだが、これもキッズクラフトコーナーに置き換えられた。現在、最も大きなセクションは野生動物の展示である。プラネタリウムはそのまま残されたが、宇宙ギャラリーはその隣に移された。

解説

改装前後の案内図について

▶ Before the refurbishment, there was a large Space Gallery close to the main entrance. However, this was changed into a café. The History Gallery, which used to be across from the Space Gallery, was also replaced by a Kids' Crafting Corner. Now, the largest section is the Wildlife Exhibit. The planetarium remained the same, but the Space Gallery was moved to be adjacent to it.

　本論1（Body 1）では、改装前後の博物館の案内図に見られる主な変化をまとめます。特に顕著な変化について触れていく必要があります。例えば、各展示室の大きさや形がどう変化したのかまで書く必要はありませんが、新しく何に変わり、何が変化していないのかを述べましょう。同じ語の繰り返しを避けるため、close→adjacentとパラフレーズするなど、多様な表現を心がけましょう。

位置の表し方

locateed in A（A に位置して）
The store is located in the south.（その店は南に位置する）
in front of A（A の前に）
The station is in front of the park.（駅は公園の前にある）
behind A（A の後ろに）
The restaurant is behind the bank.（レストランは銀行の裏にある）
next to A（A の隣に）
The café is next to the bookshop.（そのカフェは書店の隣にある）
close to A（A の近くに）
The hotel is close to the station.（そのホテルは駅の近くにある）
adjacent to A（A に隣接して）
The bakery is adjacent to the sporting goods shop.
（そのベーカリーはスポーツ用品店に隣接している）
in the vicinity of A（A の付近に）
The public toilets are in the vicinity of the shopping centre.
（その公衆トイレはショッピングセンター周辺にある）
opposite A（A の反対側に）
The zoo is opposite the primary school.
（その動物園は小学校の反対側にある）

Body 2

8 The maps below show the layout of a museum before and after it went through refurbishment. The pie charts underneath show the results of a questionnaire asking about the respective satisfaction levels of women, men, and children. Summarise the information by selecting and reporting the main features, and make comparisons where relevant.

訳 下の案内図は、ある博物館の改装前後のレイアウトを示している。その下の円グラフは、女性、男性、子ども、それぞれの満足度についてのアンケート結果を示している。主な特徴を選んで伝え、必要に応じて比較をしながら、情報をまとめなさい。

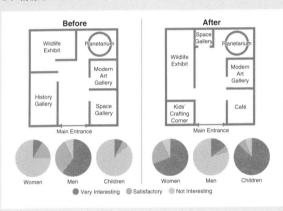

Before / After

Wildlife Exhibit / Planetarium / Modern Art Gallery / History Gallery / Space Gallery / Main Entrance

Space Gallery / Wildlife Exhibit / Planetarium / Modern Art Gallery / Kids' Crafting Corner / Café / Main Entrance

Women / Men / Children ● Very Interesting ● Satisfactory ● Not Interesting

モデルエッセーより

Before renovations were carried out, about two thirds of adult male guests were highly satisfied with the content of the museum. However, now the museum is more appealing for women and children. Close to three quarters of women said that the museum was very interesting, and more than 80% of children had the same opinion.

訳 改装が行われる前は、大人の男性客の約3分の2はこの博物館の展示内容に大変満足していた。しかし、今ではこの博物館は、女性や子どもにとってより魅力的なものになっている。4分の3近くの女性が、この博物館は大変興味深いと答え、80%超の子どもが同じ意見だった。

解説

改装前後の円グラフについて

▶ Before renovations were carried out, about two thirds of adult male guests were highly satisfied with the content of the museum. However, now the museum is more appealing for women and children. Close to three quarters of women said that the museum was very interesting, and more than 80% of children had the same opinion.

　本論2（Body 2）では、円グラフのデータについて、改装の前と後でどのような変化が見られたのかを述べています。本論1（Body 1）と本論2（Body 2）の分量に偏りが出ないように、同じくらいの語数でまとめています。ここでも円グラフに見られるすべての変化について逐一書く必要はなく、主な変化を簡潔にまとめましょう。どのような書き方をしたら語数を節約しつつたくさんの情報が組み込めるかを考えながら、描写していくのがコツです。ここでは、男性の満足度が減り、女性と子どもの満足度が上がったという変化を軸にして、具体的な数値を組み込みながら書いています。

このフレーズ、たいせつ！

☐ carry out
　行う
☐ be highly satisfied with A
　Aに大変満足している
☐ appealing for A
　Aにとって魅力的な

Conclusion

8 The maps below show the layout of a museum before and after it went through refurbishment. The pie charts underneath show the results of a questionnaire asking about the respective satisfaction levels of women, men, and children. Summarise the information by selecting and reporting the main features, and make comparisons where relevant.

訳 下の案内図は、ある博物館の改装前後のレイアウトを示している。その下の円グラフは、女性、男性、子ども、それぞれの満足度についてのアンケート結果を示している。主な特徴を選んで伝え、必要に応じて比較をしながら、情報をまとめなさい。

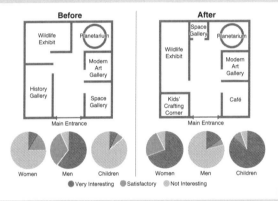

🔍 **モデルエッセーより** ||||||||||||||||||||||||||||||||||||||||||||||||||||||||||||||||||||||||||||||| |||||||||

Various changes were made to the museum, which resulted in a great shift in the satisfaction levels of customers.

訳 この博物館にはさまざまな変更が加えられ、そのことが客の満足度における大きな変化につながった。

解 説

全体の描写

▶ Various changes were made to the museum, which resulted in a great shift in the satisfaction levels of customers.

　全体的にどのような変化が見られたのか、案内図と円グラフの両方から読み取れる変化を概要的にまとめます。Task 1では結論（Conclusion）のパラグラフは必須ではないため、今回のように1文にまとめられる場合は、本論2（Body 2）に組み込んでも良いでしょう。

📖 対比する際に使えるコロケーション

☐ a clear correlation with A
　 Aとの明らかな相関
☐ no correlation can be seen in A
　 Aに相関が見られない
☐ a correlation between A and B
　 AとBの相関
☐ compared to the other
　 もう1つと比べると
☐ make a comparison
　 比較する

☐ less than a fifth of A
　 Aの20%より少ない
☐ more than two thirds of A
　 Aの3分の2より多い
☐ approximately half of A
　 Aの約半分
☐ a significant number of A
　 かなりの数のA
☐ a large proportion of A
　 Aの大半

IELTS Writing

第4章

Task 2

Task 2の心得10選

・導入と結論以外での主観的な主張は避ける

・250語以上、理想的には270語〜300語で書く

・導入は、一般文とエッセー全体の主題文で始める

・本論では、主題文で主張を述べ、支持文で主張の根拠
　を述べる

・結論では、ディスコースマーカー（discourse markers）
　を使用する

・幅広い語彙と表現を用いる

・無生物主語や受動態など、高度な文法を用いる

・指示文を2回以上読み、それに確実に答えるよう意識
　する

・エッセー全体を通して論理性（logicality）と一貫性
　（coherence）を保つ

・「議論・意見型」「賛成・反対型」「課題解決型」の出題
　パターンを把握する

9 動物がテーマの問題
Animal [Animal Testing: For or Against?]

Nowadays, animal experiments are widely used to develop new medicines and to test the safety of various products. Some people argue that these experiments should be banned because it is morally wrong to cause animals to suffer, while others are in favour of them because of their benefits to humanity. Discuss both views and give your own opinion.

⟍ Brainstorming

Introduction ▶ 指示文のパラフレーズと意見の提示をする

指示文のパラフレーズ: *some people say that animal testing is unavoidable, others say that animal testing is cruel and should be banned*

動物実験の利点: *animal testing helps to create new medicine and products that benefit society*

自分は反対の立場である: *I am against animal experiments*

Body 1 ▶ 長所をまとめる
Good Side

人間に害が少なく、大量にでき低コスト: *less harm to humans (less of a moral issue), mass experiments are possible, less cost*

Body 2 ▶ 短所をまとめる
Bad Side

動物に害を与える→他の方法を探るべき: *harms animals when the products or medicines are underdeveloped (there is still a moral issue) → there should be other ways such as testing on humans or computer simulations*

Conclusion ▶ 上記を踏まえ全体をまとめる

まとめ1: *animal testing should be banned and alternatives put to use*

まとめ2: *no animals should be forced to suffer solely for the benefit of humans*

Model Essay

Introduction

Animal experiments are often conducted to test the safety of new products and medicines before putting them to practical use on humans. Although some people say that animal testing is unavoidable for producing safe products, others argue that it is an unethical act which should be banned. I personally think that there is an urgent need to stop experiments on animals.

Body 1

Those who stand by the opinion that animal testing is necessary emphasise the following benefits. If we were to test underdeveloped products and medicines on humans, companies and researchers would have to take legal responsibility, especially if the products that they tested caused any harm. Also, many people would be reluctant to participate in such risky experiments. Compared to this, tests on animals, especially small animals such as mice and rats, can be done in mass numbers at low costs with less of a moral burden.

Body 2

Although animal experimentation does have its benefits, there are people who are more concerned about its downsides. They say that animal testing is an immoral act because many animals end up being harmed or even killed in the process. Just because the experiments are performed on animals instead of humans, it does not mean that there is less of a moral issue. Those against animal testing state that, with the advanced technology that we have today, there should be other ways to test the safety and efficacy of products, such as through computer simulations.

Conclusion

Considering both sides of this issue, I stand by the opinion that testing on animals should be banned immediately and replaced by other less harmful alternatives. No animals should be forced to suffer solely for the benefit of us human beings.

(282 words)

Introduction

9 Nowadays, animal experiments are widely used to develop new medicines and to test the safety of various products. Some people argue that these experiments should be banned because it is morally wrong to cause animals to suffer, while others are in favour of them because of their benefits to humanity. Discuss both views and give your own opinion.

訳 昨今、動物実験は新しい医薬品の開発やさまざまな製品の安全性確認のために広く行われている。動物を苦しめることは倫理的に間違っているため、このような実験は廃止されるべきであると主張する人がいる一方で、人類にとって有益であるという理由からそれら（動物実験）を支持する人もいる。（賛成派と反対派の）両方の見解について論じ、自分自身の意見を述べなさい。

 モデルエッセーより ||||||||||||||||||||||||||||||||||||||||||||||||||||||||||||||||||||||| |||||||||||

Animal experiments are often conducted to test the safety of new products and medicines before putting them to practical use on humans. Although some people say that animal testing is unavoidable for producing safe products, others argue that it is an unethical act which should be banned. I personally think that there is an urgent need to stop experiments on animals.

訳 動物実験は、新製品や医薬品を人間で実用化する前に、その安全性を確認するために実施されることが多い。安全な製品を製造するには動物実験は避けられないと言う人もいるが、禁止すべき非倫理的な行為であると主張する人もいる。私は、個人的には動物実験を中止することが急務であると考えている。

主張に使える表現

IELTS のライティングでは、論理的かつ客観的に自分の意見を述べることが重要です。I guess や I feel などの口語表現の使用は避け、客観性の高い表現を心がけましょう。

I personally think that ～　（個人的に～と思う）
I personally believe that ～　（個人的に～と考えている）
I personally recommend that ～　（個人的に～を勧める）
I stand by the opinion that ～　（～という意見を支持する）
I strongly believe that ～　（～と確信している）
I am of the opinion that ～　（～という意見である）
I support the idea that ～　（～というアイデアを支持する）
In my personal opinion, A should ～　（個人の意見としては、A は～べきである）

▶ 解 説

トピックについての一般的な事実

▶ Animal experiments are often conducted to test the safety of new products and medicines before putting them to practical use on humans.

　導入 (Introduction) 冒頭の一般文 (General Statement) では、動物実験について客観的な一般論を述べています。誰もがうなずける内容で始め、エッセー全体の主題文 (Thesis Statement) につなげます。

トピックのパラフレーズと自分の意見

▶ Although some people say that animal testing is unavoidable for producing safe products, others argue that it is an unethical act which should be banned. I personally think that there is an urgent need to stop experiments on animals.

　エッセー全体の主題文 (Thesis Statement) の1文目で、賛否両論あることを示した後、個人の意見や立場で導入をまとめます。下線部のAlthough some people say that ..., others argue that .... 「～と言う人もいるが、～と主張する人もいる」は、賛成意見と反対意見を両方提示するときに使える表現です。

この**単語**、たいせつ！

☐ experiment
　(名) 実験
☐ conduct
　(動) 行う
☐ unavoidable
　(形) 避けられない
☐ argue
　(動) 主張する

この**フレーズ**、たいせつ！

☐ test the safety
　安全性を検査する
☐ practical use
　実用
☐ unethical act
　非倫理的な行為
☐ urgent need
　急務

Body 1

9 Nowadays, animal experiments are widely used to develop new medicines and to test the safety of various products. Some people argue that these experiments should be banned because it is morally wrong to cause animals to suffer, while others are in favour of them because of their benefits to humanity. Discuss both views and give your own opinion.

訳 昨今、動物実験は新しい医薬品の開発やさまざまな製品の安全性確認のために広く行われている。動物を苦しめることは倫理的に間違っているため、このような実験は廃止されるべきであると主張する人がいる一方で、人類にとって有益であるという理由からそれら（動物実験）を支持する人もいる。（賛成派と反対派の）両方の見解について論じ、自分自身の意見を述べなさい。

🔍 モデルエッセーより ||||||||||||||||||||||||||||||||||||||||||||||||||||||||||||||||||||||||||||| |||||||||

Those who stand by the opinion that animal testing is necessary emphasise the following benefits. If we were to test underdeveloped products and medicines on humans, companies and researchers would have to take legal responsibility, especially if the products that they tested caused any harm. Also, many people would be reluctant to participate in such risky experiments. Compared to this, tests on animals, especially small animals such as mice and rats, can be done in mass numbers at low costs with less of a moral burden.

訳 動物実験は必要であるという立場を取る人たちは、以下の利点を強調している。もし、開発途中の製品や医薬品を人間で試すとしたら、試した製品が彼ら（被験者）に何らかの害を与えた場合、企業や研究者たちは法的責任を取らなければならなくなるだろう。また、多くの人はそのような危険な実験に参加することに気が進まないだろう。これに比べて、動物、特にマウスやラットなどの小さな動物を用いた実験は、低コストで倫理的負担も少なく、たくさん行うことができる。

接頭辞 under- の意味

under は「下に」という意味ですが、そこから「十分でない」という解釈も生まれます。接頭辞 under- で始まる underdeveloped は「まだ十分に発達していない」つまり「低開発の、未発達の、発育不全の」という意味になります。こうした接頭辞を含む語を活用することで、否定のニュアンスを1語の中で簡潔に表現できます。

解 説

主題文

▶ Those who stand by the opinion that animal testing is necessary emphasise the following benefits.

　本論（Body）は主題文（Topic Sentence）と支持文（Supporting Sentences）で構成されます。主題文はこのパラグラフで述べる内容をまとめたものになり、必ず本論の最初に置きます。ここでは、賛成派の意見についてこれから述べるということを明示しています。

支持文

▶ If we were to test underdeveloped products and medicines on humans, companies and researchers would have to take legal responsibility, especially if the products that they tested caused any harm. Also, many people would be reluctant to participate in such risky experiments. Compared to this, tests on animals, especially small animals such as mice and rats, can be done in mass numbers at low costs with less of a moral burden.

　支持文（Supporting Sentences）では、賛成派の意見について「人間での実験は法的責任を伴う」「危険な実験に参加したくない人も多い」「動物実験は低コストで倫理的負担が少ない」という3つの理由を挙げています。下線部のようなディスコースマーカー（discourse markers）を用いて話の展開を示唆するのがポイントです。

この単語、たいせつ！

- emphasise (動)強調する
- benefit (名)利益
- underdeveloped (形)未開発の
- legal (形)法的な

このフレーズ、たいせつ！

- take legal responsibility 法的責任を取る
- risky experiment 危険な実験
- moral burden 倫理的負担

145

Body 2

9 Nowadays, animal experiments are widely used to develop new medicines and to test the safety of various products. Some people argue that these experiments should be banned because it is morally wrong to cause animals to suffer, while others are in favour of them because of their benefits to humanity. Discuss both views and give your own opinion.

訳 昨今、動物実験は新しい医薬品の開発やさまざまな製品の安全性確認のために広く行われている。動物を苦しめることは倫理的に間違っているため、このような実験は廃止されるべきであると主張する人がいる一方で、人類にとって有益であるという理由からそれら（動物実験）を支持する人もいる。（賛成派と反対派の）両方の見解について論じ、自分自身の意見を述べなさい。

モデルエッセーより |||||||||||||||||||||||||||||||||||||||||||||||||||||||||||||||||||||||||||||||||||||||||

Although animal experimentation does have its benefits, there are people who are more concerned about its downsides. They say that animal testing is an immoral act because many animals end up being harmed or even killed in the process. Just because the experiments are performed on animals instead of humans, it does not mean that there is less of a moral issue. Those against animal testing state that, with the advanced technology that we have today, there should be other ways to test the safety and efficacy of products, such as through computer simulations.

訳 動物実験に利点があることは確かであるが、悪い点のほうを心配する人々がいる。彼らは、その過程で多くの動物が害を受けたり殺されたりすることになるため、動物実験は倫理に反する行為であると主張する。人間の代わりに動物を用いて実験を行っているからといって、倫理的な問題が少ないわけではない。動物実験に反対する人々は、今日の進歩した技術をもってすれば、製品の安全性や有効性を試す方法は、コンピューターシミュレーションのように、他にもあるはずだと言う。

 end up の意味と使い方

end up は最終的にある状態や境遇に達することを意味し、モデルエッセーでは end up -ing を「～という結果に終わる」という意味で使っています。-ing の代わりに名詞を続けることもでき、また、名詞の前に前置詞の in、with、as などを伴う場合もあります。

解 説

主題文

▶ Although animal experimentation does have its benefits, there are people who are more concerned about its downsides.

　主題文（Topic Sentence）では、譲歩を表すAlthough を用いて、動物実験には悪い点があると心配する人もいる ことを示しています。

支持文

▶ They say that animal testing is an immoral act because many animals end up being harmed or even killed in the process. Just because the experiments are performed on animals instead of humans, it does not mean that there is less of a moral issue. Those against animal testing state that, with the advanced technology that we have today, there should be other ways to test the safety and efficacy of products, such as through computer simulations.

　支持文（Supporting Sentences）では、主題文の具体 的な理由として「多くの動物が害を受けたり殺されたりす る」「倫理的な問題は少ないわけではない」「今日の進歩し た技術を使えば他の方法があるはず」といった事柄を、 主観的な表現にならないように述べています。

Conclusion

9 Nowadays, animal experiments are widely used to develop new medicines and to test the safety of various products. Some people argue that these experiments should be banned because it is morally wrong to cause animals to suffer, while others are in favour of them because of their benefits to humanity. Discuss both views and give your own opinion.

訳 昨今、動物実験は新しい医薬品の開発やさまざまな製品の安全性確認のために広く行われている。動物を苦しめることは倫理的に間違っているため、このような実験は廃止されるべきであると主張する人がいる一方で、人類にとって有益であるという理由からそれら（動物実験）を支持する人もいる。（賛成派と反対派の）両方の見解について論じ、自分自身の意見を述べなさい。

Q モデルエッセーより ||||||||||||||||||||||||||||||||||||||||||||||||||||||||||||||||||||||||||||||| ||||||||||||

Considering both sides of this issue, I stand by the opinion that testing on animals should be banned immediately and replaced by other less harmful alternatives. No animals should be forced to suffer solely for the benefit of us human beings.

訳 この問題に関する両方の立場を鑑みた上で、私は動物実験は即座に禁止されるべきであり、より害の少ない別の実験方法で置き換えられるべきであるという立場を取る。私たち人間の利益のためだけに、決して動物に苦痛を強いるべきではないのである。

 要約する際に使える表現

To sum up（要するに）
In summary（要約すると）
In conclusion（結論として）
In the end（最終的に）
As mentioned above（上記の通り）
To wrap it up（まとめると）
All things considered（すべてのことを考慮すると）
As a final point（最終のポイントとして）
Considering both sides of A（A の両側面を考慮すると）

▶ 解 説

要約文

▶ Considering both sides of this issue, I stand by the opinion that testing on animals should be banned immediately and replaced by other less harmful alternatives.

結論（Conclusion）では、文章全体のまとめとして、発展的に自分の意見を述べます。ここでは分詞構文を用いて、両方の意見について考慮した上での自分の主張を簡潔に再提示しています。

結論文

▶ No animals should be forced to suffer solely for the benefit of us human beings.

「人間の利益のためだけに動物を苦しめるべきではない」という1文で論を締めくくっています。全否定のNoを用いたNo animalsで始めることで、「1匹の動物たりとも〜ない」といった強調の表現になります。

この単語、たいせつ！

☐ ban
　⑩禁止する
☐ replace
　⑩置き換える
☐ alternative
　⑧代替案

このフレーズ、たいせつ！

☐ solely for the benefit of A
　Aの利益のためだけに

📖 動物に関連したコロケーション

☐ endangered species
　絶滅危惧種
☐ exotic animals
　外来種の動物
☐ protect flora and fauna
　動植物を守る
☐ put animals on display
　動物を展示する
☐ instinct to hunt for food
　獲物を狩る本能

☐ destroy natural habitats
　自然生息地を破壊する
☐ bear healthy offspring
　健康な子孫を生む
☐ create a wildlife reserve
　野生生物保護区を造る
☐ a highly evolved animal
　高度に進化した動物
☐ wildlife conservation
　野生生物保護

10 ロボットがテーマの問題
Robot [Robots: Good or Bad for Society?]

Some people think that robots are very important for future human development. Others, however, think that robots are dangerous inventions that could have negative effects on society. Discuss both views and give your opinion.

Brainstorming

Introduction 指示文のパラフレーズと意見の提示をする

指示文のパラフレーズ：*robots help humans with various tasks and benefit humans in many ways / however, if we are not careful, they could pose a major threat to our society*

注意深く使えば社会の利益に：*I personally think that robots can be beneficial to our society as long as they are used morally and with great care*

Body 1 長所をまとめる
Good Side

①工場などの単純作業に役立つ：*help us get jobs done faster and more efficiently* → *faster for robots to do menial, repetitive jobs such as manufacturing in factories* → *robots do not get tired so they can work constantly and efficiently*

②力仕事などに役立つ：*help us to complete tasks that we otherwise cannot accomplish* → *jobs that require great strength such as lifting and transporting things*

Body 2 短所をまとめる
Bad Side

①故障する：*robots sometimes break down (large system failures or hacking) and it takes time to repair the damage*

②ハッキングのリスク：*another serious risk is hacking* → *hackers can steal confidential information and cause the robots to malfunction*

Conclusion 上記を踏まえ全体をまとめる

まとめ1：*robots are necessary in our society*

まとめ2：*they will continue to evolve and benefit us as long as we are aware of the dangers and consider them when we invent new robots*

Model Essay

Introduction

Robots assist humans with various tasks and benefit mankind in many ways. However, some people fear that if we are not fully aware of their risks and downsides, robots can pose a major threat to our society. I personally believe that robots can be highly beneficial to our society as long as they are used cautiously.

Body 1

Robots are beneficial to society since they help us to complete tasks more efficiently and with higher accuracy. For example, robots are excellent for working in manufacturing plants since they can do menial jobs that require repetitive movements without getting tired or losing concentration. They can also assist us in tasks that require great strength such as lifting and transporting heavy things. This makes jobs like construction work, transporting heavy luggage, or even caregiving less of a burden for humans.

Body 2

Technological innovations definitely make our society more convenient and boost the economy, but it is essential for us to acknowledge the fact that if we do not use these inventions wisely, they may be used against us and become a major threat. Robots are highly vulnerable to technical difficulties and system failures. One error in the system can cause a massive breakdown, and it often takes a lot of time to repair the damage. Another serious risk is hacking. If a hacker finds their way into the computers controlling the robots, they can steal confidential information and cause the robots to malfunction.

Conclusion

In conclusion, there are both benefits and dangers concerning the widespread use of robots. However, our society has become highly dependent on robots and we have reached a point at which our world cannot function without them. Robots are necessary in today's society, and they will continue to evolve and benefit humanity as long as we take precautions against certain dangers.

(299 words)

Introduction

10 Some people think that robots are very important for future human development. Others, however, think that robots are dangerous inventions that could have negative effects on society. Discuss both views and give your opinion.

訳 今後の人類の発展のためにロボットは非常に重要だと考える人がいる。しかし、その一方で、ロボットは社会に悪い影響をもたらし得る危険な発明であると考える人もいる。両方の見解について論じ、自分の意見を述べなさい。

モデルエッセーより ||||||||||||||||||||||||||||||||||||||||||||||||||||||||||||||||||||||||||||||||||||||||||| |||||||||

Robots assist humans with various tasks and benefit mankind in many ways. However, some people fear that if we are not fully aware of their risks and downsides, robots can pose a major threat to our society. I personally believe that robots can be highly beneficial to our society as long as they are used cautiously.

訳 ロボットは人間がさまざまな仕事をこなすのを手助けし、多くの点で人類に利益をもたらす。しかし、私たちが十分にその危険性や悪い点を認識していなければ、ロボットは社会に重大な脅威を与え得るのではないかと恐れる人もいる。私は個人的には、ロボットは慎重に使われれば、私たちの社会にとって非常に有益なものになると考える。

▶ 解 説

トピックについての一般的な事実

▶ Robots assist humans with various tasks and benefit mankind in many ways.

　今回は、議論・意見型のエッセーです。まず、誰もがうなずける一般的な事実を述べます。この文は、ロボットが人類に多くの利益をもたらすことを伝えていると同時に、指示文の前半部分のパラフレーズにもなっています。このように、一般的な事実を交えながら、指示文をパラフレーズしていくという方法もあります。

トピックのパラフレーズと自分の意見

▶ However, some people fear that if we are not fully aware of their risks and downsides, robots can pose a major threat to our society. I personally believe that robots can be highly beneficial to our society as long as they are used cautiously.

　ここでの1文目は、指示文の2文目のパラフレーズです。ロボットの危険性を指摘している人たちがいることを伝えています。続く文の下線部で、意見を表明しています。ただし、ここでは単に賛成・反対という立場を示すのでなく、「慎重に使えば」社会にとってロボットは有益なものになるという、条件つきの意見となっています。現代社会で起こっている多くの問題は、単に賛成・反対だけでは割り切れないものが非常に多いため、「○○である限り」や「○○されれば」などと条件や譲歩をつけ加えて自分の立場を述べるというのも、1つの方法です。

この**単語**、たいせつ！

- [ ] assist
  - (動) 手助けする
- [ ] benefit
  - (動) 利益を与える
- [ ] fear
  - (動) 恐れる
- [ ] beneficial
  - (形) 有益な
- [ ] cautiously
  - (副) 用心深く

この**フレーズ**、たいせつ！

- [ ] various tasks
  - さまざまな仕事
- [ ] pose a major threat to A
  - Aに重大な脅威を与える

Body 1

10 Some people think that robots are very important for future human development. Others, however, think that robots are dangerous inventions that could have negative effects on society. Discuss both views and give your opinion.

訳 今後の人類の発展のためにロボットは非常に重要だと考える人がいる。しかし、その一方で、ロボットは社会に悪い影響をもたらし得る危険な発明であると考える人もいる。両方の見解について論じ、自分の意見を述べなさい。

 モデルエッセーより ||||||||||||||||||||||||||||||||||||||||||||||||||||||||||||||||||||||||||||||| |||||||||||

Robots are beneficial to society since they help us to complete tasks more efficiently and with higher accuracy. For example, robots are excellent for working in manufacturing plants since they can do menial jobs that require repetitive movements without getting tired or losing concentration. They can also assist us in tasks that require great strength such as lifting and transporting heavy things. This makes jobs like construction work, transporting heavy luggage, or even caregiving less of a burden for humans.

訳 ロボットはより効率的にかつより正確に作業を終わらせる手助けをしてくれるので、社会にとって有益である。例えば、ロボットは疲れたり集中力を切らしたりすることなく、同じ動作の繰り返しを要する単純作業を行うことができるため、製造工場で働くことに非常に向いている。また、それら（ロボット）は重い物を持ち上げたり運んだりするなどといった大きな力を要する作業を行う際にも手助けしてくれる。これによって、建設作業、重い荷物の運搬、さらには介護などの仕事も、人間にとって負担の少ないものになる。

💬 require の使い方

「必要とする」という意味の require という語の成り立ちは re（強調）＋ quire（求める）であり、「何かをするために強く求める」というニュアンスがあります。need（必要とする）や necessary（必要な）の言い換えとして、アカデミックライティングでよく使われる語です。require を用いることで無生物主語の文を作ることができるため、客観性の高い表現が可能です。例えば、Academic papers require outside sources.（学術論文には外部の情報が必要である）や Attendance is required in this class.（このクラスでは出席が必須である）のような使い方ができます。名詞の requirement は「必要条件」という意味になり、satisfy the requirement（必要条件を満たす）や meet the minimum requirement（最低限の必要条件を満たす）のように使えます。これらはフレーズごと覚えておきましょう。

▶ 解 説

主題文

▶ Robots are beneficial to society since they help us to complete tasks more efficiently and with higher accuracy.

　本論1（Body 1）では、最初に賛成派の意見を展開します。理由を述べるsinceに続くハイライト部分で、ロボットが有益である理由を簡潔にまとめています。

支持文

▶ For example, robots are excellent for working in manufacturing plants since they can do menial jobs that require repetitive movements without getting tired or losing concentration. They can also assist us in tasks that require great strength such as lifting and transporting heavy things. This makes jobs like construction work, transporting heavy luggage, or even caregiving less of a burden for humans.

　For example以下では、ロボットが有益である理由を具体的に述べています。ロボットは集中力を切らさずに単純作業を行うことができる、さらに荷物を運搬したり介護の負担を減らしたりする、といった例を挙げています。

この単語、たいせつ！

- [ ] efficiently
  　㊐効率的に
- [ ] accuracy
  　㊑正確さ
- [ ] repetitive
  　㊒繰り返しの
- [ ] transport
  　㊓運ぶ
- [ ] caregiving
  　㊑介護
- [ ] burden
  　㊑負担

このフレーズ、たいせつ！

- [ ] complete tasks
  　作業を終わらせる
- [ ] with higher accuracy
  　より高い精度で
- [ ] menial job
  　単純な作業
- [ ] lose concentration
  　集中力を失う

「具体例」に関する表現

支持文では、主題文で行った主張を強化します。その際、example（具体例）、explanation（説明）、experience（経験）、evidence（証拠）の「4つのE」を効果的に活用しましょう。無関係な例ではなく妥当な例を提示できているか、注意を払いましょう。ここでは具体例を提示するときに使える表現を紹介します。

A good example of this is 〜 .（これの良い例は〜である）
A good illustration of this is 〜 .（これの良い実例は〜である）
One specific example of this is 〜 .（これに関する具体的な例の1つに〜がある）
One intriguing fact about A is 〜 .（Aに関する興味をそそる事実の1つに〜がある）
One notable example can be found in 〜 .（1つの顕著な例は〜に見つけられる）

Body 2

10 Some people think that robots are very important for future human development. Others, however, think that robots are dangerous inventions that could have negative effects on society. Discuss both views and give your opinion.

訳 今後の人類の発展のためにロボットは非常に重要だと考える人がいる。しかし、その一方で、ロボットは社会に悪い影響をもたらし得る危険な発明であると考える人もいる。両方の見解について論じ、自分の意見を述べなさい。

🔍 モデルエッセーより ||||||||||||||||||||||||||||||||||||||||||||||||||||||||||||||||||||||||||||||||||||||||||||||||||||| ||||||||||||

Technological innovations definitely make our society more convenient and boost the economy, but it is essential for us to acknowledge the fact that if we do not use these inventions wisely, they may be used against us and become a major threat. Robots are highly vulnerable to technical difficulties and system failures. One error in the system can cause a massive breakdown, and it often takes a lot of time to repair the damage. Another serious risk is hacking. If a hacker finds their way into the computers controlling the robots, they can steal confidential information and cause the robots to malfunction.

訳 技術的な革新が私たちの社会をより便利にし、経済を活性化させることは確かであるが、これらの発明は、賢く使わなければ、私たちに不利な使用となり、大きな脅威になり得るかもしれないと認識することが必要不可欠である。ロボットは技術的な不具合やシステムエラーに対して非常に脆弱である。システム内で1つでもエラーが起こると、大規模な故障を引き起こすことがあり、しばしば修復に多くの時間を要する。もう1つの大きなリスクがハッキングである。もしハッカーがロボットを管理しているパソコンに侵入したら、彼らは機密情報を盗んだり、ロボットを誤作動させたりすることができる。

 ## Task 2 で使える副詞

IELTS のライティング Task 2 でも、高得点を狙うためには副詞の使用が重要ですが、always や definitely などは今回のように強調を示唆する場合以外は客観性を欠く表現となります。断定的な副詞の使用は原則として避け、以下のようなものを使いましょう。

highly（高く）	primarily（主に）	potentially（潜在的に）
widely（広く）	currently（現在は）	comparatively（比較的）
strongly（強く）	relatively（比較的）	critically（極めて）

▶ 解 説

主題文

▶ Technological innovations definitely make our society more convenient and boost the economy, but it is essential for us to acknowledge the fact that if we do not use these inventions wisely, they may be used against us and become a major threat.

　本論2（Body 2）では反対派の意見を述べますが、主題文では、内容が賛成派の意見から反対派の意見に急に変わらないよう、ワンクッションを設けています。本論1（Body 1）の内容を簡潔にまとめた上で、後半のbut以下でこれに反する内容を述べています。

支持文

▶ Robots are highly vulnerable to technical difficulties and system failures. One error in the system can cause a massive breakdown, and it often takes a lot of time to repair the damage. Another serious risk is hacking. If a hacker finds their way into the computers controlling the robots, they can steal confidential information and cause the robots to malfunction.

　ハイライト部分が2つの理由になります。1つ目の理由については、続く下線部で具体的に説明をしています。2つ目の理由についても、続く下線部で、ハッキングが起こったとしたら具体的にどのような被害が及ぶのかについて説明しています。

この**単語**、たいせつ！

- [ ] definitely
  副確かに
- [ ] convenient
  形便利な
- [ ] essential
  形必要不可欠な
- [ ] acknowledge
  動認める
- [ ] wisely
  副賢く
- [ ] vulnerable
  形脆弱な
- [ ] malfunction
  動誤作動する

この**フレーズ**、たいせつ！

- [ ] technological innovation
  技術革新
- [ ] boost the economy
  経済を活性化させる
- [ ] massive breakdown
  大規模な故障
- [ ] steal confidential information
  機密情報を盗む

Conclusion

10 Some people think that robots are very important for future human development. Others, however, think that robots are dangerous inventions that could have negative effects on society. Discuss both views and give your opinion.

訳 今後の人類の発展のためにロボットは非常に重要だと考える人がいる。しかし、その一方で、ロボットは社会に悪い影響をもたらし得る危険な発明であると考える人もいる。両方の見解について論じ、自分の意見を述べなさい。

 モデルエッセーより ‖‖

In conclusion, there are both benefits and dangers concerning the widespread use of robots. However, our society has become highly dependent on robots and we have reached a point at which our world cannot function without them. Robots are necessary in today's society, and they will continue to evolve and benefit humanity as long as we take precautions against certain dangers.

訳 結論として、ロボットが広く使用されることに関しては利益と危険性の両方が伴う。しかしながら、私たちの社会はロボットに大きく頼るようになってきており、世界はロボットなしでは機能し得ない地点にまで達している。ロボットは今日の社会において必要なものであり、私たちがある種の危険性に対する予防策を取っている限りは、それら（ロボット）は進化し続け、人類に利益をもたらし続けるであろう。

💬 条件の表現

副詞節を導く従位接続詞の働きをする as long as は、「条件や限度」を表し、「～する限り」「～である限り」などと訳されます。類似の表現に if only（～さえすれば）があります。以下の例文を比較分析してみましょう。

- **as long as（～である限り）**
I am happy as long as I have money. （お金がある限り私は幸せである）
- **if only（～さえすれば）**
I would be happy if only I had money. （お金さえあれば幸せなのに）

解 説

要約文

▶ In conclusion, there are both benefits and dangers concerning the widespread use of robots. However, our society has become highly dependent on robots and we have reached a point at which our world cannot function without them.

下線部で文章全体をまとめ、ハイライト部分で発展的に現在の状況を述べています。その上で、この後の部分では自分の意見を再度述べています。

結論文

▶ Robots are necessary in today's society, and they will continue to evolve and benefit humanity as long as we take precautions against certain dangers.

導入（Introduction）で述べた自分の意見をより具体的にまとめ、さらに下線部で、条件を表す副詞節を用いて控えめに自分の意見を締めくくっています。

この単語、たいせつ！

- function
  働 機能する
- necessary
  形 必要な
- evolve
  働 進化する
- humanity
  名 人類

このフレーズ、たいせつ！

- widespread use of robots
  ロボットの広い使用
- become highly dependent on robots
  ロボットに大きく頼るようになる
- take precautions
  予防策を取る

📖 ロボットに関連したコロケーション

- rely on robots
  ロボットに依存する
- exceed human efficiency
  人間の効率を超える
- replace humans with machines
  人間を機械に置き換える
- supersede human abilities
  人間の能力を超える
- utilise artificial intelligence
  人工知能を利用する
- improve immature technology
  未発達な技術を改善する
- consider moral issues
  倫理的な問題を考慮する
- face catastrophic consequences
  壊滅的な結果に直面する
- pose a threat to our civilisation
  我々の文明に危険をもたらす
- set up an innovative company
  革新的な会社を設立する

11 テクノロジーがテーマの問題
Technology [Online Dating: For or Against?]

Recent technological advancements have made online dating popular. Consider both the positive and negative aspects of online dating and state your own opinion on it using examples.

ᐟ Brainstorming

Introduction ▶ 指示文のパラフレーズと意見の提示をする

指示文のパラフレーズ: *the advanced technology that we use today such as smartphones, computers and the internet make online dating easy and therefore more popular, especially among the youth*

直接会うほうが良い: *online dating has both advantages and disadvantages, but I personally prefer (recommend) that people date in person rather than online*

Body 1 ▶ 長所をまとめる

Pros
① どこでも可能: *can date anywhere* → *in the comfort of one's home, long distance relationships are possible, may be helpful for people with health issues*
② 経済的: *less financially demanding*

Body 2 ▶ 短所をまとめる

Cons
① 関係が簡単に切れてしまう: *makes it easy for people to cut off relationships when they go wrong* → *can simply delete or block the other person's contact details or not answer their texts or calls*
② 話の真偽が見極めにくい: *since you do not meet the person in real life, it can be hard to discern whether they are telling the truth about their identity and feelings* → *may well be faking their identity, or may have other intentions than getting into a romantic relationship* → *may result in more people getting caught up in crime*

Conclusion ▶ 上記を踏まえ全体をまとめる

まとめ1: *people should stick to the traditional way of dating in person to create intimate, long-lasting relationships*
まとめ2: *should be aware that although online dating may be convenient, it has its risks and downsides*

Model Essay

Introduction

The advanced technology that we use today makes online dating easy. Therefore, online dating has gained a great deal of popularity in recent years. Dating online has both its advantages and disadvantages, but I personally recommend that people should date in person rather than in the virtual world.

Body 1

The most significant advantage of online dating would be that it can be done anywhere. With a smartphone or computer, couples can talk with each other in the comfort of their own homes. Another benefit of online dating is that it does not cost any money. When going out on a date with someone in person, there is a need to pay for the coffee you have at a café or the film you see at the cinema. However, online dating is less financially demanding since the only things you need are your smartphone or computer and an internet connection.

Body 2

Although online dating has many benefits, we must also be fully aware of its downsides. A negative point about online dating is that it makes it easier for people to cut off relationships when they go wrong. If one person feels that the relationship is no longer beneficial, they can simply break it off by deleting or blocking the other person's contact details. Also, since you do not meet your date in person, it can be hard to discern whether they are telling the truth about their identity or feelings. For all you know, your dream date could be trying to take advantage of the personal information they manage to get out of you.

Conclusion

Online dating may be convenient and beneficial in some ways. However, I strongly believe that people should stick to the traditional style of dating in person because face-to-face interaction is the key to building long and strong relationships.

(300 words)

Introduction

11 Recent technological advancements have made online dating popular. Consider both the positive and negative aspects of online dating and state your own opinion on it using examples.

訳 近年の技術の進歩により、オンライン交際の人気が高まってきた。オンライン交際の良い面と悪い面の両方を考慮して、具体例を用いながら、これ（オンライン交際）について自分自身の意見を述べなさい。

 モデルエッセーより ||||||||||||||||||||||||||||||||||||||||||||||||||||||||||||||||||||||||||||||||||||||||| |||||||||||

The advanced technology that we use today makes online dating easy. Therefore, online dating has gained a great deal of popularity in recent years. Dating online has both its advantages and disadvantages, but I personally recommend that people should date in person rather than in the virtual world.

訳 私たちが現在利用している先進的な技術により、オンライン交際がしやすくなっている。そのため、ここ数年間でオンライン交際は非常に人気が高まってきている。オンライン上で交際をすることには長所と短所の両方があるが、私は個人的には、バーチャル世界で交際をするよりも、直接会う形を勧める。

「長所と短所」の表し方

Task 2 の賛成・反対型エッセーでは、物事の長所と短所を描写するスキルが求められます。以下のような表現を覚えて活用しましょう。ちなみに、長所を述べる際には It seems advantageous that ～ . （～は有利であると思われる）や The main advantage of A is that ～ . （A の主な長所は～である）などの表現も便利です。

benefits and drawbacks（利点と欠点）
strengths and weaknesses（強みと弱み）
merits and demerits（メリットとデメリット）
advantages and disadvantages（長所と短所）
positive and negative aspects（良い面と悪い面）

解 説

トピックについての一般的な事実

▶ The advanced technology that we use today makes
online dating easy. Therefore, online dating has
gained a great deal of popularity in recent years.

　一般文（General Statement）では、オンライン交際に
おける誰もがうなずける事柄を述べます。オンライン交際
の人気が高まっていることを、become popularよりも高
度な表現gain a great deal of popularityを用いて伝えて
います。

トピックのパラフレーズと自分の意見

▶ Dating online has both its advantages and
disadvantages, but I personally recommend that
people should date in person rather than in the
virtual world.

　指示文のpositive and negative aspects（良い面と悪
い面）をadvantages and disadvantagesとパラフレーズ
し、オンライン交際には長所と短所があることを認めなが
ら、バーチャルよりも直接会う形での交際を勧めるという
自分の意見を述べています。このように、エッセー全体の
主題文（Thesis Statement）ではエッセーの要点を簡潔
にまとめる必要があるので、具体例や詳細は本論（Body）
で述べましょう。

この単語、たいせつ！

☐ advantage
　(名)利点
☐ recommend
　(動)勧める

このフレーズ、たいせつ！

☐ advanced
　technology
　先進的な技術
☐ virtual world
　仮想世界

Body 1

11 Recent technological advancements have made online dating popular. Consider both the positive and negative aspects of online dating and state your own opinion on it using examples.

訳 近年の技術の進歩により、オンライン交際の人気が高まってきた。オンライン交際の良い面と悪い面の両方を考慮して、具体例を用いながら、これ（オンライン交際）について自分自身の意見を述べなさい。

🔍 **モデルエッセーより** ||||||||||||||||||||||||||||||||||||||||||||||||||||||||||||||||||||||||||

The most significant advantage of online dating would be that it can be done anywhere. With a smartphone or computer, couples can talk with each other in the comfort of their own homes. Another benefit of online dating is that it does not cost any money. When going out on a date with someone in person, there is a need to pay for the coffee you have at a café or the film you see at the cinema. However, online dating is less financially demanding since the only things you need are your smartphone or computer and an internet connection.

訳 オンライン交際の最大の利点は、どこでもそれを行うことができる点だろう。スマートフォンかパソコンさえあれば、カップルは自宅で心地よく過ごしながらお互いと会話することができる。オンライン交際のもう1つの利点は、お金がかからない点である。誰かと直接会ってデートをするときは、カフェで飲むコーヒーや映画館で見る映画の代金を支払わなければならない。しかしオンライン交際は、スマートフォンかパソコン、それにインターネット接続しか必要としないため、経済的な負担が少ないのである。

 映画に関する表現

「映画」を表す語として知られているものに、アメリカ英語の movie とイギリス英語の film があります。movie には、アクション映画やロマンス映画などの商業的なコンテンツといったニュアンスも含まれます。一方、film は、芸術的・学術的な文脈で映画を語る際によく使われます。また、「映画館」は、アメリカ英語では movie theater、イギリス英語では cinema が一般的に使われます。関連語として cinematography（映画撮影術）も覚えておきましょう。また、subtitles（字幕）、dubbing（吹き替え）、trailer（予告編）なども頻出表現です。

▶解 説

主題文

▶ The most significant advantage of online dating
would be that it can be done anywhere.

　本論1（Body 1）では、賛成派の意見を理由とともに簡
潔に述べています。

支持文

▶ With a smartphone or computer, couples can talk
with each other in the comfort of their own homes.
Another benefit of online dating is that it does not
cost any money. When going out on a date with
someone in person, there is a need to pay for the
coffee you have at a café or the film you see at the
cinema. However, online dating is less financially
demanding since the only things you need are
your smartphone or computer and an internet
connection.

　ハイライトした部分が賛成派の意見です。下線部では、
それの裏づけとなる具体的な事例を挙げています。ハイラ
イト部分だけでは話が漠然としており読み手に伝わりづら
いのですが、下線部のような具体的な話を入れることで、
言いたいことを読み手に理解してもらえるようになり、説
得力も増します。

Body 2

11 Recent technological advancements have made online dating popular. Consider both the positive and negative aspects of online dating and state your own opinion on it using examples.

訳 近年の技術の進歩により、オンライン交際の人気が高まってきた。オンライン交際の良い面と悪い面の両方を考慮して、具体例を用いながら、これ（オンライン交際）について自分自身の意見を述べなさい。

🔍 モデルエッセーより ||||||||||||||||||||||||||||||||||||||||||||||||||||||||||||||||||||||||||||||||||| ||||||||||||

Although online dating has many benefits, we must also be fully aware of its downsides. A negative point about online dating is that it makes it easier for people to cut off relationships when they go wrong. If one person feels that the relationship is no longer beneficial, they can simply break it off by deleting or blocking the other person's contact details. Also, since you do not meet your date in person, it can be hard to discern whether they are telling the truth about their identity or feelings. For all you know, your dream date could be trying to take advantage of the personal information they manage to get out of you.

訳 オンライン交際には多くの利点があるが、私たちはその悪い点も十分に認識していなければならない。オンライン交際の悪い点は、うまくいかなくなったときに、関係を絶ちやすい点であろう。一方が（2人の）関わり合いにこれ以上利益がないと感じたら、相手の連絡先を削除したりブロックしたりすることで、簡単に人と別れることができてしまうのである。さらに交際相手と直接会わないため、相手が自らの人物像や気持ちに関して、真実を述べているか見極めるのが難しい場合がある。ことによると、あなたの理想の交際相手が、あなたから引き出すことに成功した個人情報を悪用しようとしているかもしれないのだ。

 「見極める」の表し方

discern は「感覚や知性で見極める」という意味の語で、「注意深い判断・理解を伴う」といったニュアンスを持ち、discern right from wrong（善悪を見分ける）のように、discern A from B の形で使うことができます。より頻出の類義語 distinguish（区別して見分ける）も、同様に distinguish A from B の形で使い、tell A from B とパラフレーズ可能です。関連語に「区別する」という意味の differentiate や discriminate があります。differentiate は differentiate between right and left（左右を区別する）のように、前置詞 between を伴って使い、2つの物事の相違点を区別することに重きを置くニュアンスになります。discriminate には「差別する」という意味もあり、ネガティブな意味で使われることもあります。

166

▶ 解 説

主題文

▶ Although online dating has many benefits, we must
also be fully aware of its downsides.

　主題文（Topic Sentence）では、オンライン交際には
多くの利点があるものの悪い点も認識しなければならない
ことについて述べ、これから反対派の意見を展開すること
を示唆しています。

支持文

▶ A negative point about online dating is that it
makes it easier for people to cut off relationships
when they go wrong. If one person feels that
the relationship is no longer beneficial, they can
simply break it off by deleting or blocking the other
person's contact details. Also, since you do not
meet your date in person, it can be hard to discern
whether they are telling the truth about their identity
or feelings. For all you know, your dream date
could be trying to take advantage of the personal
information they manage to get out of you.

　ハイライト部分が反対派の意見です。下線部では、本
論1（Body 1）のように具体的な事例を挙げてハイライト
部分を補足するというよりは、一般的に言われている事実
を挙げてハイライト部分の内容をより詳細に説明する形を
取っています。主題文での主張を強化するには example
（具体例）、explanation（説明）、experience（経験）、
evidence（証拠）の「4つのE」が有効です。

この**単語**、たいせつ!

☐ discern
　⑩見極める

この**フレーズ**、たいせつ!

☐ cut off
　relationships
　縁を切る
☐ go wrong
　うまくいかなくなる
☐ personal
　information
　個人情報

Conclusion

11 Recent technological advancements have made online dating popular. Consider both the positive and negative aspects of online dating and state your own opinion on it using examples.

訳 近年の技術の進歩により、オンライン交際の人気が高まってきた。オンライン交際の良い面と悪い面の両方を考慮して、具体例を用いながら、これ（オンライン交際）について自分自身の意見を述べなさい。

🔍 モデルエッセーより ||||||||||||||||||||||||||||||||||||||||||||||||||||||||||||||||||||||||||||||

Online dating may be convenient and beneficial in some ways. However, I strongly believe that people should stick to the traditional style of dating in person because face-to-face interaction is the key to building long and strong relationships.

訳 オンライン交際はいくつかの点においては便利で有益であるかもしれない。しかし、私は対面での交流が長く続く強固な関係を築く鍵であるため、人々は従来の直接会って交際するスタイルを守り続けるべきであると確信している。

 「関係」についての表現

この部分では、「長く続く強固な関係性を構築する」を build long and strong relationships とシンプルな単語の組み合わせで表現していますが、評価基準の「語彙力（Lexical Resource）」においてより高得点を狙うなら、以下のような表現が可能です。

form stable and solid ties（安定的で強固な絆を形成する）
forge enduring and robust bonds（不変で堅固な結びつきを構築する）
establish lasting and resilient connections（長続きし、回復力のあるつながりを構築する）
develop profound and long-lasting partnerships（深く長続きする相互関係を発展させる）

▶ 解 説

要約文

▶ Online dating may be convenient and beneficial in some ways.

結論（Conclusion）では、まず1文目でオンライン交際に利点があるかもしれないと認め、続く部分で反対派という自分の立場を展開していきます。50%程度の可能性を意味するmayを用いることで、この後の主張にうまくつなげています。

結論文

▶ However, I strongly believe that people should stick to the traditional style of dating in person because face-to-face interaction is the key to building long and strong relationships.

下線部で自分の主張を明確に述べ、ハイライト部分でその理由を発展的に補足し、まとめています。

この**単語**、たいせつ！

- convenient
  形 便利な
- beneficial
  形 有益な

この**フレーズ**、たいせつ！

- stick to the traditional style
  従来のスタイルに固執する
- face-to-face interaction
  対面での交際
- build long and strong relationships
  長く強固な関係を構築する

📖 技術に関連したコロケーション

- introduce a new machine
  新しい機械を導入する
- invent the computer
  パソコンを発明する
- add a new feature
  新しい機能をつけ加える
- design an application
  アプリをデザインする
- generate electricity
  電気を作り出す

- emergence of new technology
  新しい技術の出現
- cutting-edge technology
  最先端の技術
- become rapidly obsolete
  急速に廃れる
- access to the internet
  インターネットのアクセス
- work from home
  在宅で仕事をする

12 健康がテーマの問題
Health [Healthcare for Free: For or Against?]

Each individual should be held fully responsible for their own health, so governments should not be responsible for covering the medical fees of their people. To what extent do you agree or disagree with this statement?

Brainstorming

Introduction 指示文のパラフレーズと意見の提示をする

指示文のパラフレーズ: *some people stand by the opinion that individuals should be responsible for managing their own health and governments should not have to cover individuals' medical fees*

医療費が安価すぎると人々が健康に対して無責任に: *it is understandable that people may become less responsible for their health if medical fees are set too low*

しかし政府が一部でも負担するべき: *however, I think the government should pay for at least a part of medical fees*

Body 1 1つ目の理由をまとめる

社会経済的地位の低い人が困る: *if the government does not give financial support, people with low socioeconomic status will not be able to get the care that they need* → *often it is these people who need the most medical care because of malnutrition and jobs that are harmful to health*

Body 2 2つ目の理由をまとめる

生まれつきの病気を持つ人が困る: *some people are just born with certain conditions or are vulnerable to certain sicknesses* → *it is not their fault, so they should not have to bear the entire burden* → *for example, although colds are said to be preventable, some people may be born with a weaker than average immune system* → *it would be unfair for innately more vulnerable people to have to pay expenses*

Body 3 3つ目の理由をまとめる

個人が置かれた状況によるリスクもある: *where an individual lives and/or their type of job (lifestyle) may put them at a higher risk of certain medical conditions* → *e.g. people who live in large cities are exposed to more air pollution and are therefore prone to a higher risk of respiratory conditions*

Conclusion 上記を踏まえ全体をまとめる

まとめ1: *medical care should not be completely free*

まとめ2: *people should have to cover part of their own medical costs* → *cost should not be overly cheap that people become irresponsible, but costs should be affordable/accessible to most people*

Model Essay

Introduction

Some believe that individuals should be held responsible for managing their own physical well-being and claim that people should have to pay fully for any healthcare they receive. They believe medical care should not be provided completely for free, since this may cause people to take less care of managing their health. However, I strongly believe the government should still cover part of their people's medical fees as a form of social welfare.

Body 1

Medical treatment is often extremely expensive. If governments did not provide financial support to pay for healthcare, people with low socioeconomic status would not be able to receive medication. It is impoverished people who need the most medical care since they more often develop malnutrition and are exposed to unhealthy working environments which have negative effects on their health.

Body 2

Furthermore, some people have innate health problems or are born with different deficiencies which make them more vulnerable to certain sicknesses. In such cases, it would not be fair for these people to have to pay high medical costs in order to receive sufficient treatment. They are not at fault for their chronic health conditions, so the government should support their well-being through financial aid.

Body 3

Finally, many people develop certain health issues due to their living environments. For example, people who live in large cities may be more prone to respiratory problems. In addition, those living in remote areas with unhygienic conditions may be more likely to be affected by infectious diseases. It is often difficult for individuals to prevent or avoid maladies caused by their surrounding environment, so it is only fair that governments help treat these sicknesses.

Conclusion

Governments should be responsible for protecting the well-being of their people by providing healthcare to everyone at an affordable price. Therefore, they should cover a reasonable proportion of people's medical expenses. (302 words)

Introduction

12 Each individual should be held fully responsible for their own health, so governments should not be responsible for covering the medical fees of their people. To what extent do you agree or disagree with this statement?

訳 各個人が自分の健康について全責任を負うべきであるので、政府は国民の医療費の一部負担の責任を持つべきではない。あなたはこの意見にどの程度賛成あるいは反対しますか？

🔍 モデルエッセーより ||||||||||||||||||||||||||||||||||||||||||||||||||||||||||||||||||||||||||||||||| |||||||||||

Some believe that individuals should be held responsible for managing their own physical well-being and claim that people should have to pay fully for any healthcare they receive. They believe medical care should not be provided completely for free, since this may cause people to take less care of managing their health. However, I strongly believe the government should still cover part of their people's medical fees as a form of social welfare.

訳 各個人は、自分の体の健康管理に対して責任を負うべきであり、自身の受けるあらゆる治療の費用全額を支払うべきであると考える人もいる。彼らは、人々の健康管理に対する注意低下につながりかねないので、医療は完全に無償で提供されるべきではない、と考えている。しかし、私は、それでも政府は社会福祉の1つとして国民の医療費の一部を負担するべきであると確信している。

▶ 解 説

トピックについての一般的な事実

▶ Some believe that individuals should be held responsible for managing their own physical well-being and claim that people should have to pay fully for any healthcare they receive. They believe medical care should not be provided completely for free, since this may cause people to take less care of managing their health.

まず指示文のパラフレーズを行っています。その後に、医療費を完全に無償化すると自分の健康管理に注意を払わなくなる人がいるという一般論かつ背景知識を展開しています。

トピックのパラフレーズと自分の意見

▶ However, I strongly believe the government should still cover part of their people's medical fees as a form of social welfare.

エッセー全体の主題文（Thesis Statement）では、その前の内容を踏まえて、「政府は国民の医療費の（全額ではなく）一部を負担するべきである」という自分の立場を明らかにしています。この問題では、政府が国民の医療費を負担すべきかどうかについての賛成・反対だけでなく、負担の度合いについての意見も述べることになります。ここでは、政府は国民の医療費を部分的に負担するべきであるという意見を提示しています。

Body 1

12 Each individual should be held fully responsible for their own health, so governments should not be responsible for covering the medical fees of their people. To what extent do you agree or disagree with this statement?

訳 各個人が自分の健康について全責任を負うべきであるので、政府は国民の医療費の一部負担の責任を持つべきではない。あなたはこの意見にどの程度賛成あるいは反対しますか？

モデルエッセーより ||||||||||||||||||||||||||||||||||||||||||||||||||||||||||||||||||||||||||||||||||||||||||||||| ||||||||||

Medical treatment is often extremely expensive. If governments did not provide financial support to pay for healthcare, people with low socioeconomic status would not be able to receive medication. It is impoverished people who need the most medical care since they more often develop malnutrition and are exposed to unhealthy working environments which have negative effects on their health.

訳 医療は非常に高額である場合が多い。もし、政府が医療費を支払うための経済的援助を提供しなければ、社会経済的地位の低い人々は、薬による治療を受けられないだろう。最も医療を必要としているのは、栄養失調になったり、健康に悪影響を及ぼす不健全な労働環境にさらされたりすることが多い貧困層の人々なのである。

💬 nutrition（栄養）の関連表現

malnutrition は mal（悪い）＋ nutrition（栄養）つまり「栄養失調」を表します。nutrition の派生語には、形容詞の nutritional（栄養上の）と nutritious（栄養のある）、副詞の nutritionally（栄養上で）などがあります。形容詞 nutritional と nutritious の意味の違いは、address a nutritional deficiency（栄養不足に対処する）や Nutritious vegetables are expensive.（栄養価の高い野菜は値段が高い）といったフレーズや短めの文で覚えておきましょう。他の関連語に nutrient があり、「栄養になる」という意味の形容詞、もしくは「栄養物」という意味の名詞として使われます。また、nutrition と同語源の語に、nurse（看護師）、nursery（託児所）、nurture（育てる）、nourish（養う）などがあります。

解 説

本論1（Body 1）では、政府が国民の医療費を部分的に負担すべきであるという主張の1つ目の理由である「貧困層の人々が適切な医療を受けられなくなる」ということについて書いています。主題文で1つ目の理由を述べ、支持文でそれを具体的に補足しています。

主題文

▶ Medical treatment is often extremely expensive. If governments did not provide financial support to pay for healthcare, people with low socioeconomic status would not be able to receive medication.

1つ目の理由を述べる前に、その背景にある「医療費が非常に高額である場合が多い」という現実に触れています。often を用いることで断定を避けています。続く文で、医療費が高額であることの影響を大きく受ける人々について書いています。

支持文

▶ It is impoverished people who need the most medical care since they more often develop malnutrition and are exposed to unhealthy working environments which have negative effects on their health.

貧困層の人々への配慮が必要である理由を、下線部のIt isで始まる強調構文を用いて説明しています。「貧困層の人ほど健康問題を抱えやすい」という現状を述べることで、主張を裏づけています。自分の意見をしっかりと補強していく流れを作ることが大切です。

この**単語**、たいせつ！

- extremely
  剾 非常に
- medication
  名 薬物治療
- malnutrition
  名 栄養不足

この**フレーズ**、たいせつ！

- medical treatment
  治療
- provide financial support
  経済的援助を提供する
- low socioeconomic status
  低い社会経済的な地位
- impoverished people
  貧困層の人々

Body 2

12 Each individual should be held fully responsible for their own health, so governments should not be responsible for covering the medical fees of their people. To what extent do you agree or disagree with this statement?

訳 各個人が自分の健康について全責任を負うべきであるので、政府は国民の医療費の一部負担の責任を持つべきではない。あなたはこの意見にどの程度賛成あるいは反対しますか？

モデルエッセーより ‖‖‖ ‖‖‖‖‖‖‖

Furthermore, some people have innate health problems or are born with different deficiencies which make them more vulnerable to certain sicknesses. In such cases, it would not be fair for these people to have to pay high medical costs in order to receive sufficient treatment. They are not at fault for their chronic health conditions, so the government should support their well-being through financial aid.

訳 それに加えて、生まれつきの健康問題を抱えている人や、生まれ持ったさまざまな欠陥により、特定の病気にかかりやすくなっている人もいるのである。そのような場合、こうした人々が十分な治療を受けるために高額の医療費を支払わなければならないのは不公平だろう。彼らの慢性的な健康問題は本人たちのせいではないのだから、政府は経済的な援助を通して、彼らの健康を支えるべきである。

 ### 病気に関する表現

健康不良や病名など、病気に関する語には、以下のようなものがあります。

sickness（健康が悪い状態にあること）	cancer（癌）
illness（身体・精神の状態が良くないこと）	asthma（喘息）
disease（医学的に診断可能な病気）	pneumonia（肺炎）
deficiency（体内で必要な物質が不足している状態）	arthritis（関節炎）
ailment（比較的軽い慢性的な病気）	stroke（脳卒中）
malady（慢性病などの深刻な病気）	migraine（偏頭痛）
disorder（身体・精神が正常に機能しない状態）	epilepsy（てんかん）
affliction（心身の苦痛）	measles（麻疹）
hypertension（高血圧）	chickenpox（水疱瘡）
diabetes（糖尿病）	

▶ 解説

主題文

▶ Furthermore, some people have innate health problems or are born with different deficiencies which make them more vulnerable to certain sicknesses.

　主題文では、Furthermore というディスコースマーカーを用いて、2つ目の理由である「生まれつきの健康問題やさまざまな欠陥を抱えている人もいる」ということを提示しています。

支持文

▶ In such cases, it would not be fair for these people to have to pay high medical costs in order to receive sufficient treatment. They are not at fault for their chronic health conditions, so the government should support their well-being through financial aid.

　そして支持文では、主題文について詳細に説明をしています。生まれつきの健康問題や欠陥を抱えている場合、その治療のために高額な医療費を払わなくてはならないのは不平等であり、政府が経済的な援助をする必要があると述べています。

この単語、たいせつ！

☐ deficiency
　㊑欠陥

このフレーズ、たいせつ！

☐ have innate health problems
　生まれつき健康問題がある
☐ sufficient treatment
　十分な治療
☐ chronic health conditions
　慢性的な健康状態
☐ financial aid
　財政援助

Body 3

12 Each individual should be held fully responsible for their own health, so governments should not be responsible for covering the medical fees of their people. To what extent do you agree or disagree with this statement?

訳 各個人が自分の健康について全責任を負うべきであるので、政府は国民の医療費の一部負担の責任を持つべきではない。あなたはこの意見にどの程度賛成あるいは反対しますか?

モデルエッセーより ||||||||||||||||||||||||||||||||||||||||||||||||||||||||||||||||||||||||||||||||||||||||||||| ||||||||||||

Finally, many people develop certain health issues due to their living environments. For example, people who live in large cities may be more prone to respiratory problems. In addition, those living in remote areas with unhygienic conditions may be more likely to be affected by infectious diseases. It is often difficult for individuals to prevent or avoid maladies caused by their surrounding environment, so it is only fair that governments help treat these sicknesses.

訳 最後に、多くの人々は生活環境が原因で特定の健康問題を抱えるのである。例えば、大都市に住んでいる人は、呼吸器系の疾患をより引き起こしやすいかもしれない。また、衛生的でない環境で遠隔地に暮らしている人は、感染症にかかる可能性がより高いかもしれない。周囲の環境によってもたらされる病気を個人が予防したり避けたりすることは困難なことが多いので、政府がこれらの病気の治療を手助けすることこそが公正なのである。

「傾向」の表現

ここでは、be prone to respiratory problems (呼吸器系の疾患を引き起こしやすい) や be more likely to be affected by infectious diseases (感染症にかかる可能性が高い) といった表現で、病気にかかりやすい傾向を表現しています。be prone to は、この例のように、病気などネガティブな文脈での「傾向」について使われます。be likely to は「何かが起こる可能性が高い」ときに使われ、名詞の likelihood (見込み、可能性) も、IELTS ライティングの頻出語です。類似の表現である be inclined to は、「性質や嗜好、意思によってその方向に傾いている」ことを意味します。また tend to は、頻繁に起こる傾向を指して使われ、名詞 tendency (傾向) を用いた have a tendency to に言い換え可能です。

解 説

主題文

▶ Finally, many people develop certain health issues due to their living environments.

ここでは、3つ目の理由である「多くの人は生活環境によって健康問題を抱える」ということを提示しています。そして、続く支持文で具体的な説明をしています。

支持文

▶ For example, people who live in large cities may be more prone to respiratory problems. In addition, those living in remote areas with unhygienic conditions may be more likely to be affected by infectious diseases. It is often difficult for individuals to prevent or avoid maladies caused by their surrounding environment, so it is only fair that governments help treat these sicknesses.

「生活環境によって健康問題を抱える」だけでは、イメージがわきづらいですよね。そのため、下線部のように具体例を挙げて補足しています。これらの説明は、医療についての専門的な知識がなくても、見聞きしたことなど一般的な常識の範囲内で可能です。

この単語、たいせつ!

- [ ] develop
   動 (病気に) かかる
- [ ] respiratory
   形 呼吸器系の
- [ ] malady
   名 病気

このフレーズ、たいせつ!

- [ ] remote area
   遠隔地
- [ ] unhygienic conditions
   衛生的でない状態
- [ ] infectious disease
   感染病

 ライティングの評価基準

IELTS のライティングは、以下の項目がそれぞれ 0.5 刻みの 9 段階で採点されます（p. 16 の表も参照してください）。
まず、Task 1 には「課題の達成度（Task Achievement）」、Task 2 には「課題への回答（Task Response）」という、問題や指示文に確実に回答しているかの項目があります。また、「内容の一貫性（Coherence and Cohesion）」で高評価を得るには、しっかりした構成と、ディスコースマーカー（接続表現）の使用が重要です。「語彙力（Lexical Resource）」では、高頻出語彙だけでなく、幅広い表現や難易度の高い語彙を適切に使えているかが評価されます。そして「文法知識と正確さ（Grammatical Range and Accuracy）」の項目では、複雑な文法や構文を適切かつ正確に使うことで高得点を狙えます。

Conclusion

12 Each individual should be held fully responsible for their own health, so governments should not be responsible for covering the medical fees of their people. To what extent do you agree or disagree with this statement?

訳 各個人が自分の健康について全責任を負うべきであるので、政府は国民の医療費の一部負担の責任を持つべきではない。あなたはこの意見にどの程度賛成あるいは反対しますか？

 モデルエッセーより ||||||||||||||||||||||||||||||||||||||||||||||||||||||||||||||||||||||||||||||||||||||||||||||||

Governments should be responsible for protecting the well-being of their people by providing healthcare to everyone at an affordable price. Therefore, they should cover a reasonable proportion of people's medical expenses.

訳 政府は、あらゆる人に手の届く値段で医療を提供することを通して、国民の健康を守る責任を持つべきである。従って、政府は人々の医療費のうち妥当な割合を負担するべきである。

❗ 結論のディスコースマーカー

結論（Conclusion）のパラグラフでは、全体のまとめを示唆するディスコースマーカー（discourse markers）を用いることで、エッセーの論旨が分かりやすくなります。以下の表現は、p. 148 で紹介した「要約する際に使える表現」と同様、本論（Body）で展開した議論をまとめることを示唆するものです。ただし In a nutshell のような口語的な決まり文句や、冗長になり得る It can be concluded that 〜などの使用は避けたほうが良い場合もあります。

Overall（概して）
Therefore（それゆえ）
Consequently（結果的に）
All in all（大体において）
Last but not least（最後に）
All things considered（万事を考慮して）

解説

要約文

▶ Governments should be responsible for protecting the well-being of their people by providing healthcare to everyone at an affordable price.

　3つの異なる理由すべてに共通する内容で、論をまとめています。結論（Conclusion）を書く際には、どれか1つの本論（Body）の内容に偏り過ぎず、ここまでの内容をうまく網羅する形でまとめていきましょう。

結論文

▶ Therefore, they should cover a reasonable proportion of people's medical expenses.

　最後に、「政府は人々の医療費の一部を負担すべきである」という自分の意見を、導入（Introduction）とは異なる言い回しで繰り返して、締めくくっています。

この単語、たいせつ！

☐ reasonable
　㊝妥当な

このフレーズ、たいせつ！

☐ protect the well-being
　健康を守る
☐ at an affordable price
　手頃な値段で
☐ medical expenses
　医療費

健康に関連したコロケーション

☐ take a pill
　薬を飲む
☐ catch a cold
　風邪をひく
☐ prescribe medicine
　薬を処方する
☐ eat a balanced diet
　バランスの取れた食事をする
☐ work out regularly
　定期的に運動する
☐ die of lung cancer
　肺がんで亡くなる
☐ take painkillers
　痛み止めを飲む
☐ suffer from depression
　うつ病を患う
☐ symptoms of coronavirus
　コロナウイルスの症状
☐ develop a mental illness
　精神的な病気になる

Task 2

13 環境がテーマの問題
Environment [Fossil Fuels or Alternative Energy?]

Many countries use fossil fuels such as coal, oil, and natural gases as their main source of energy. However, in some countries, the use of alternative sources of energy such as wind and solar power is dominant. Consider the benefits and drawbacks of both fossil fuels and alternative energy and state your opinion on which type of energy should be more widely used.

Brainstorming

Introduction ▶ 指示文のパラフレーズと意見の提示をする

指示文のパラフレーズ : *majority of the world's countries use fossil fuels, but alternative sources of energy are starting to be more widely used*

代替エネルギーの使用を促すべき : *both have their pros and cons, but I believe that alternative energy is more beneficial and its usage should be encouraged as much as possible*

Body 1 ▶ 1つ目の選択肢の長所と短所をまとめる

fossil fuels *used in most countries, especially less developed countries*

Pros 低コストで新しい施設が不要 : *low cost → do not require building new facilities (can use the facilities that are already developed)*

Cons ①環境や人に有害 : *harmful to the environment → especially the fact that burning fossil fuels releases gases that are harmful to human health and cause global warming*

②枯渇する : *exhaustible → if we use them up, there will be no more left*

Body 2 ▶ 2つ目の選択肢の長所と短所をまとめる

alternative energy *used in fewer countries, especially in developed countries*

Pros ①害が少ない : *less harmful to people and the environment in that they do not release toxic gases*

②枯渇しない : *inexhaustible → just need maintenance of facilities*

Cons 高コストで新しい施設が必要 : *high cost → need to build new facilities & need people who have the technical skills to maintain them*

Conclusion ▶ 上記を踏まえ全体をまとめる

まとめ1 : *usage of alternative energy sources should be encouraged because they are more environmentally friendly and can be used for a much longer period of time*

まとめ2 : *although the cost may be higher than using fossil fuels, the cost is unavoidable for us to create and leave a sustainable society for following generations*

Model Essay

Introduction

To this day, the majority of the energy used by humans is produced by fossil fuels. However, with the advancement of technology, alternative sources of energy such as wind power, hydro power, and solar power are gradually beginning to become more widely used. Both fossil fuels and alternative energy have their pros and cons, but I believe that the use of alternative energy sources should be advanced more.

Body 1

Fossil fuels have long sustained our industries and economy. The majority of the world's countries, especially developing countries, still use them as their main source of power. The most significant benefit of fossil energy is that it can be produced at relatively low costs, using the facilities and technology that are already at hand. However, the downside is that the burning of coal, oil, and other fossil fuels releases gases that are harmful to the human body and the environment, and also speeds up global warming. On top of this, these energy sources are exhaustible, meaning that they will one day run out.

Body 2

In contrast, alternative energy sources are used to great effect mostly in developed countries. Alternative energy is beneficial since no toxic gases are released into the atmosphere during its production. Sources such as wind, water, and the sun are inexhaustible, so their usage is unlimited. On the other hand, the cost for producing renewable energy is quite expensive. This is especially true because there is a need to build high-tech facilities and to train people to run and maintain them.

Conclusion

Considering both the positive and negative aspects of fossil fuels and alternative energy, I still believe that the use of alternative energy should be encouraged so that we can leave behind a sustainable and environmentally friendly society for following generations.

(291 words)

Introduction

13 Many countries use fossil fuels such as coal, oil, and natural gases as their main source of energy. However, in some countries, the use of alternative sources of energy such as wind and solar power is dominant. Consider the benefits and drawbacks of both fossil fuels and alternative energy and state your opinion on which type of energy should be more widely used.

訳 多くの国が、石炭、石油、天然ガスなどの化石燃料を主なエネルギー源として使用している。しかし、風力や太陽光などの代替エネルギー源の使用を主とする国もある。化石燃料と代替エネルギー両方の利点と欠点を考慮し、より広く使われるべきなのはどちらかについて、自分の意見を述べなさい。

 モデルエッセーより ||||||||||||||||||||||||||||||||||||||||||||||||||||||||||||||||||||||||||||||||||||| |||||||||||

To this day, the majority of the energy used by humans is produced by fossil fuels. However, with the advancement of technology, alternative sources of energy such as wind power, hydro power, and solar power are gradually beginning to become more widely used. Both fossil fuels and alternative energy have their pros and cons, but I believe that the use of alternative energy sources should be advanced more.

訳 今日まで、人間が使うエネルギーの大部分は化石燃料によって生産されている。しかし、技術の進歩に伴い、風力、水力、太陽光などの代替エネルギーが次第に広く使用されるようになり始めている。化石燃料と代替エネルギーのどちらにも良い点と悪い点があるが、私は代替エネルギー源の使用をさらに進めていくべきだと考えている。

「進歩」に関する表現

advancement（進歩）は、科学技術や医療などにおける改善や向上を表すのによく使われます。動詞の advance（進める、進む）は「知識や研究が進歩する」ことを指し、形容詞の advanced は「技術などが進んだ」や「学問や語学が上級の」を意味します。類義語の progress（進歩、進歩する）は、前に進む過程に重きを置いた語です。pro は「前」、gress は「進む」を表し、同語源の語に grade（成績）や regress（退行する）があります。ちなみに IELTS Progress Check という公式の IELTS オンライン練習試験があるので、本番前に受けてみると良いでしょう。

▶ 解 説

トピックについての一般的な事実

▶ To this day, the majority of the energy used by humans is produced by fossil fuels. However, with the advancement of technology, alternative sources of energy such as wind power, hydro power, and solar power are gradually beginning to become more widely used.

今回は議論・意見型のエッセーです。指示文が非常に長く、すべての要素を言い換えることはできません。指示文をよく読み、重要な部分を見極める必要があります。ここでは、1文目で誰もがうなずける一般的事実を述べ、2文目で指示文のパラフレーズをしています。

トピックのパラフレーズと自分の意見

▶ Both fossil fuels and alternative energy have their pros and cons, but I believe that the use of alternative energy sources should be advanced more.

ここでは、エッセー全体にわたる議論を示唆しながら、下線部で自分の主張を明確に述べています。

この単語、たいせつ!

☐ majority
　 (名) 大部分
☐ advancement
　 (名) 進歩

このフレーズ、たいせつ!

☐ fossil fuel
　 化石燃料
☐ alternative
　 sources of
　 energy
　 代替エネルギー

Body 1

13 Many countries use fossil fuels such as coal, oil, and natural gases as their main source of energy. However, in some countries, the use of alternative sources of energy such as wind and solar power is dominant. Consider the benefits and drawbacks of both fossil fuels and alternative energy and state your opinion on which type of energy should be more widely used.

訳 多くの国が、石炭、石油、天然ガスなどの化石燃料を主なエネルギー源として使用している。しかし、風力や太陽光などの代替エネルギー源の使用を主とする国もある。化石燃料と代替エネルギー両方の利点と欠点を考慮し、より広く使われるべきなのはどちらかについて、自分の意見を述べなさい。

🔍 モデルエッセーより ‖‖‖ ‖‖‖‖‖‖‖

Fossil fuels have long sustained our industries and economy. The majority of the world's countries, especially developing countries, still use them as their main source of power. The most significant benefit of fossil energy is that it can be produced at relatively low costs, using the facilities and technology that are already at hand. However, the downside is that the burning of coal, oil, and other fossil fuels releases gases that are harmful to the human body and the environment, and also speeds up global warming. On top of this, these energy sources are exhaustible, meaning that they will one day run out.

訳 化石燃料は長きにわたり私たちの産業と経済を支えてきた。世界の大半の国々、特に発展途上国では、今でも化石燃料を主要なエネルギー源として使用している。化石エネルギーの最も大きな利点は、すでに手近にある施設や技術を使って、比較的低いコストで生産できる点である。しかし、欠点として、石炭、石油、その他の化石燃料を燃やすと人体や環境に有害なガスが排出され、地球温暖化も加速させる点が挙げられる。これに加えて、これらのエネルギー源は枯渇してしまうもの、つまり、いずれは尽きるものである。

▶ 解 説

主題文

▶ Fossil fuels have long sustained our industries and economy. The majority of the world's countries, especially developing countries, still use them as their main source of power.

化石燃料と代替エネルギーそれぞれの良い点と悪い点を考慮した上で、自分の意見を書く必要があります。本論1（Body 1）では、化石燃料について論じます。

支持文

長所（1つ）

▶ The most significant benefit of fossil energy is that it can be produced at relatively low costs, using the facilities and technology that are already at hand.

良い点として、下線部で生産コストの低さを挙げています。the most significant benefitというフレーズは、あらゆるテーマに使えるのでぜひ覚えましょう。

短所（2つ）

▶ However, the downside is that the burning of coal, oil, and other fossil fuels releases gases that are harmful to the human body and the environment, and also speeds up global warming. On top of this, these energy sources are exhaustible, meaning that they will one day run out.

悪い点として、有害なガスを発するということと、いずれ枯渇するということを挙げています。自分の意見は「化石燃料ではなく代替エネルギーの使用を促進していくべき」というものなので、化石燃料については悪い点のほうを1つ多く挙げています。ハイライト部分はディスコースマーカーの役割を果たしています。

この単語、たいせつ！

☐ sustain
　働 維持する

☐ exhaustible
　形 枯渇し得る

このフレーズ、たいせつ！

☐ at a relatively low cost
　比較的安いコストで

☐ release gas
　ガスを排出する

☐ run out
　枯渇する

Body 2

13 Many countries use fossil fuels such as coal, oil, and natural gases as their main source of energy. However, in some countries, the use of alternative sources of energy such as wind and solar power is dominant. Consider the benefits and drawbacks of both fossil fuels and alternative energy and state your opinion on which type of energy should be more widely used.

訳 多くの国が、石炭、石油、天然ガスなどの化石燃料を主なエネルギー源として使用している。しかし、風力や太陽光などの代替エネルギー源の使用を主とする国もある。化石燃料と代替エネルギー両方の利点と欠点を考慮し、より広く使われるべきなのはどちらかについて、自分の意見を述べなさい。

Ｑ モデルエッセーより ‖‖ ‖‖‖‖‖‖‖‖‖

In contrast, alternative energy sources are used to great effect mostly in developed countries. Alternative energy is beneficial since no toxic gases are released into the atmosphere during its production. Sources such as wind, water, and the sun are inexhaustible, so their usage is unlimited. On the other hand, the cost for producing renewable energy is quite expensive. This is especially true because there is a need to build high-tech facilities and to train people to run and maintain them.

訳 対照的に、代替エネルギー源はほとんどの場合、先進国で利用されて大きな効果を挙げている。代替エネルギーが有益なのは、その生産中に有害なガスが大気中に排出されないためである。風、水、太陽光などの資源は枯渇しないため、その利用に制限はない。しかしながら、その一方で、再生可能エネルギーの生産コストはかなり高額である。それは特に、先進的な技術を使用した施設を建てたり、それらの施設を運営し、維持する人材を育成したりしなければならないといった理由においてである。

解 説

主題文

▶ In contrast, <u>alternative energy sources</u> are used to great effect mostly in developed countries.

　本論2（Body 2）では代替エネルギーの良い点と悪い点について書いています。このパラグラフでは代替エネルギーを取り上げることを、冒頭で明記しています。そして、本論1（Body 1）と対比させるために、代替エネルギーがどのような国で使われているのかについて書いています。2つのBodyの構成や内容が鏡のように対比的になっていると、読み手にとっても流れが追いやすくなります。

支持文
長所（2つ）

▶ <u>Alternative energy is beneficial since no toxic gases are released into the atmosphere during its production.</u> Sources such as wind, water, and the sun are inexhaustible, so <u>their usage is unlimited.</u>

　代替エネルギーの良い点として、有害なガスが排出されないことと利用に制限がないことを、下線部で挙げています。

短所（1つ）

▶ On the other hand, <u>the cost for producing renewable energy is quite expensive.</u> This is especially true because there is a need to build high-tech facilities and to train people to run and maintain them.

　代替エネルギーの悪い点として、生産コストの高さに下線部で触れた後、2文目で主な理由を述べています。

この単語、たいせつ！

- [ ] atmosphere
  ㊂大気
- [ ] unlimited
  ㊡限られていない

この フレーズ、たいせつ！

- [ ] toxic gas
  有害なガス
- [ ] produce renewable energy
  再生可能エネルギーを生産する

Conclusion

13 Many countries use fossil fuels such as coal, oil, and natural gases as their main source of energy. However, in some countries, the use of alternative sources of energy such as wind and solar power is dominant. Consider the benefits and drawbacks of both fossil fuels and alternative energy and state your opinion on which type of energy should be more widely used.

訳 多くの国が、石炭、石油、天然ガスなどの化石燃料を主なエネルギー源として使用している。しかし、風力や太陽光などの代替エネルギー源の使用を主とする国もある。化石燃料と代替エネルギー両方の利点と欠点を考慮し、より広く使われるべきなのはどちらかについて、自分の意見を述べなさい。

モデルエッセーより ||||||||||||||||||||||||||||||||||||||||||||||||||||||||||||||||||||||||||| |||||||||||||

Considering both positive and negative aspects of fossil fuels and alternative energy, I still believe that the use of alternative energy should be encouraged so that we can leave behind a sustainable and environmentally friendly society for following generations.

訳 化石燃料と代替エネルギーの良い面と悪い面の両方を考慮すると、私はやはり、持続可能で環境に優しい社会を次世代に残していくために、代替エネルギーの使用が奨励されるべきであると考える。

解 説

要約文

▶ Considering both positive and negative aspects of fossil fuels and alternative energy,

ここまでの部分で、化石燃料と代替エネルギーそれぞれの良い点と悪い点を書いてきたので、ここでそのことに触れています。

結論文

▶ I still believe that the use of alternative energy should be encouraged so that we can leave behind a sustainable and environmentally friendly society for following generations.

前半部分では導入（Introduction）で述べた自分の意見を再度簡潔にまとめ、後半部分（下線部）ではそれを未来の展望へとつなげています。

この単語、たいせつ！

☐ encourage
　(動) 促進する
☐ sustainable
　(形) 持続可能な

このフレーズ、たいせつ！

☐ environmentally friendly
　環境に優しい
☐ for following generations
　次世代のために

環境に関連したコロケーション

☐ protect natural resources
　天然資源を守る
☐ provide technological aid
　技術的な支援を提供する
☐ conserve endangered species
　絶滅危惧種を保護する
☐ serious air pollution
　深刻な大気汚染
☐ contaminate the ocean
　海を汚染する
☐ release carbon dioxide
　二酸化炭素を排出する
☐ destroy the ozone layer
　オゾン層を破壊する
☐ enhance the greenhouse effect
　温室効果を促進させる
☐ cause climate change
　気候変動を引き起こす
☐ restore the natural environment
　自然環境を回復させる

Task 2

14 交通がテーマの問題
Transport [Low-Price Airlines: For or Against?]

Low-price airlines are becoming increasingly popular. Although these airlines do not provide the conveniences of more expensive airlines, they allow people to get to their destinations at lower costs. Discuss both the positive and negative aspects of low-price airlines and state your opinion.

Brainstorming

Introduction ▶ 指示文のパラフレーズと意見の提示をする

指示文のパラフレーズ : *more and more people are using low-price airlines for travel → although such airlines may be more accessible because of their low cost, there are both advantages and disadvantages*

格安航空は有益 : *I personally think that low-price airlines can be highly beneficial*

Body 1 ▶ 長所をまとめる
Positive Side

①より多くの人に旅と新しい経験を提供 : *allow more people to travel (even people who are not so wealthy, students) → allow more people to get new experiences and broaden their perspective*

②旅先で他のことにお金を使える : *allow travellers to use their money on other aspects of travel → can stay at better hotels, try more different kinds of food, go touring more*

Body 2 ▶ 短所をまとめる
Negative Side

①サービスが他より良くない : *the service is often not as good as that of other airlines → e.g. may not have TV or music, meals may be simpler, seats may be smaller and uncomfortable*

②安全性が犠牲になる : *safety is sometimes put at stake → low prices mean less income to company, which leads to reducing employees or overworking them with less pay → may cause serious human errors that affect the safety of flights → there are actually many cases of airline accidents conenected to low-price airlines*

Conclusion ▶ 上記を踏まえ全体をまとめる

まとめ : *low cost airlines can be extremely beneficial as long as the prices are reasonably set to benefit both the company and its customers (not so high that airline travel becomes an extreme luxury but not so low that it is not beneficial for workers)*

Model Essay

Introduction

Low-price airlines are increasing significantly in both numbers and popularity. Although these airlines may be more accessible to people for their low cost, there are both advantages and disadvantages when using them for travel. I personally think that low-price airlines can be highly beneficial for the future of air travel.

Body 1

One of the biggest advantages of low-cost air travel is that it allows more people the opportunity to travel. Thanks to such airlines, flying to many destinations is no longer an unaffordable luxury. Allowing more people to travel means that they can experience new places and cultures and broaden their perspective. Low air travel costs also mean that people can spend the money that they save on other aspects of travel. For example, they can use it to stay at better hotels, try different kinds of local food, or visit more tourist spots.

Body 2

However, the reality of low-cost airlines is not all rainbows and butterflies. The service that cheap airlines provide is often not as good as that of more expensive flights. Low-cost airlines often do not have TVs or music, serve simple meals, and the seats may be smaller and more uncomfortable. Another severe downside of these airlines is that safety is sometimes put at stake. Tight flight schedules or overwork of employees with insufficient pay may contribute to keeping the price of airplane tickets down, but they may also sometimes result in maintenance errors which may lead to fatal accidents.

Conclusion

Taking both the advantages and disadvantages of low-cost airlines into consideration, I stand by the opinion that these airlines can be beneficial as long as the prices are reasonably moderated so as not to impose an excessive burden on either the customers or employees.

(286 words)

Introduction

14 Low-price airlines are becoming increasingly popular. Although these airlines do not provide the conveniences of more expensive airlines, they allow people to get to their destinations at lower costs. Discuss both the positive and negative aspects of low-price airlines and state your opinion.

訳 格安航空の人気が高まってきている。これらの航空会社は、より高額な航空会社ほどの利便性は提供しないが、格安で目的地にたどり着くことを可能にする。格安航空の良い面と悪い面の両方を論じ、自分の意見を述べなさい。

モデルエッセーより ||||||||||||||||||||||||||||||||||||||||||||||||||||||||| |||||||||

Low-price airlines are increasing significantly in both numbers and popularity. Although these airlines may be more accessible to people for their low cost, there are both advantages and disadvantages when using them for travel. I personally think that low-price airlines can be highly beneficial for the future of air travel.

訳 格安航空は、数も人気も著しく増大している。これらの航空会社は、費用の安さの点で、人々にとってより手が届きやすいかもしれないが、これら（の航空会社）を旅行に使用するに当たっては、長所と短所の両方がある。私は個人的には、未来の空の旅において、格安航空は非常に有益になり得ると考える。

 賛成・反対に関する表現

I partially agree with A. （私は部分的に A に賛成である）
I agree with the fact that ～ . （私は～という事実に賛成である）
I am against the idea that ～ . （私は～という考えに反対である）
I completely disagree with A. （私は完全に A に反対である）
Those who disagree with the opinion are ～ . （その意見に反対する人々は～である）
There are some opponents who disagree with the idea. （そのアイデアに反対する人もいる）

解 説

トピックについての一般的な事実

▶ Low-price airlines are increasing significantly in both numbers and popularity.

　ここでは、格安航空の人気が近年高まってきており、その数も増えてきているという、誰もがうなずける今日の状況を述べています。

トピックのパラフレーズと自分の意見

▶ Although these airlines may be more accessible to people for their low cost, there are both advantages and disadvantages when using them for travel. I personally think that low-price airlines can be highly beneficial for the future of air travel.

　下線部では、譲歩の表現を用いて、長所も短所もあることを述べ、最後の文では自分の意見を述べています。ヘッジング（hedging）と呼ばれる表現であるmayやcanを用いることで、控えめさを出し、断定的になるのを避けています。

この単語、たいせつ！

- accessible
  圏（経済的に）手が届く

このフレーズ、たいせつ！

- low-price airlines
  格安航空
- increase significantly
  顕著に増える
- highly beneficial
  非常に有益である

Body 1

14 Low-price airlines are becoming increasingly popular. Although these airlines do not provide the conveniences of more expensive airlines, they allow people to get to their destinations at lower costs. Discuss both the positive and negative aspects of low-price airlines and state your opinion.

訳 格安航空の人気が高まってきている。これらの航空会社は、より高額な航空会社ほどの利便性は提供しないが、格安で目的地にたどり着くことを可能にする。格安航空の良い面と悪い面の両方を論じ、自分の意見を述べなさい。

モデルエッセーより ||||||||||||||||||||||||||||||||||||||||||||||||||||||||||||||||||| |||||||||||

One of the biggest advantages of low-cost air travel is that it allows more people the opportunity to travel. Thanks to such airlines, flying to many destinations is no longer an unaffordable luxury. Allowing more people to travel means that they can experience new places and cultures and broaden their perspective. Low air travel costs also mean that people can spend the money that they save on other aspects of travel. For example, they can use it to stay at better hotels, try different kinds of local food, or visit more tourist spots.

訳 格安航空の最大の長所の1つは、より多くの人に旅の機会が与えられる点である。そうした航空会社のおかげで、さまざまな目的地に飛行機で行くことは、もはや手の届かない贅沢ではない。より多くの人にとって旅が可能になるということは、彼らが新しい場所や文化を体験し、視野を広げられることを意味する。航空運賃が安いということは、人々が浮いたお金を旅の他の要素に使えるということでもある。例えば、彼らはそれ（浮いたお金）を、より良いホテルに宿泊したり、さまざまな地元料理を食べてみたり、より多くの観光名所を訪れたりすることに使うことができるのだ。

▶ 解 説

主題文

▶ One of the biggest advantages of low-cost air travel is that it allows more people the opportunity to travel.

　本論1（Body 1）では、格安航空支持派の意見を述べています。主題文（Topic Sentence）で、このパラグラフでは格安航空の利点を挙げていくことを明記しています。

支持文

▶ Thanks to such airlines, flying to many destinations is no longer an unaffordable luxury. Allowing more people to travel means that they can experience new places and cultures and broaden their perspective. Low air travel costs also mean that people can spend the money that they save on other aspects of travel. For example, they can use it to stay at better hotels, try different kinds of local food, or visit more tourist spots.

　1つ目の要素については、より多くの人が旅の機会を持てる→視野を広げられる、と少し発展させて述べています。このように、より多くの人が旅行できるようになることで、どのような効果が期待できるのかまで具体的に書けると、説得力が増します。2つ目の要素については、ハイライト部分のother aspects of travelとは具体的にどのようなものを指すのかについて、続く下線部で詳しく補足しています。この2つの下線部のように具体例を挙げられると、読み手もイメージしやすくなります。

この単語、たいせつ！

- [ ] opportunity
  名機会
- [ ] destination
  名目的地
- [ ] luxury
  名贅沢品
- [ ] aspects
  名要素

このフレーズ、たいせつ！

- [ ] thanks to A
  Aのおかげで
- [ ] broaden one's perspective
  視野を広げる

Body 2

14 Low-price airlines are becoming increasingly popular. Although these airlines do not provide the conveniences of more expensive airlines, they allow people to get to their destinations at lower costs. Discuss both the positive and negative aspects of low-price airlines and state your opinion.

訳 格安航空の人気が高まってきている。これらの航空会社は、より高額な航空会社ほどの利便性は提供しないが、格安で目的地にたどり着くことを可能にする。格安航空の良い面と悪い面の両方を論じ、自分の意見を述べなさい。

モデルエッセーより ||||||||||||||||||||||||||||||||||||||||||||||||||||||||||||||||||||||||||||||||||||||||||||| |||||||||

However, the reality of low-cost airlines is not all rainbows and butterflies. The service that cheap airlines provide is often not as good as that of more expensive flights. Low-cost airlines often do not have TVs or music, serve simple meals, and the seats may be smaller and more uncomfortable. Another severe downside of these airlines is that safety is sometimes put at stake. Tight flight schedules or overwork of employees with insufficient pay may contribute to keeping the price of airplane tickets down, but they may also sometimes result in maintenance errors which may lead to fatal accidents.

訳 しかしながら、格安航空の現実は良いことばかりではない。安い航空会社が提供するサービスは、より高額な航空便のサービスほどは良くないことが多い。格安航空は多くの場合、テレビや音楽がついておらず、出てくる食事が簡素で、座席がより小さくて快適でない可能性がある。これらの航空会社のもう1つの深刻な欠点は、時に安全性が犠牲にされかねない点である。立て込んだ飛行スケジュールや、不十分な給料での従業員の過剰労働は、航空券の値段を安く保つことには貢献するかもしれない。しかしこれらは、致命的な事故につながる可能性がある整備ミスも、時として引き起こすかもしれないのだ。

▶ 解 説

主題文

▶ However, the reality of low-cost airlines is not all rainbows and butterflies.

　格安航空の現実は良いことばかりではないと述べることによって、これから本論1（Body 1）で展開した格安航空の良い点とは反対の「悪い点」について書く、ということを示しています。

支持文

▶ The service that cheap airlines provide is often not as good as that of more expensive flights. Low-cost airlines often do not have TVs or music, serve simple meals, and the seats may be smaller and more uncomfortable. Another severe downside of these airlines is that safety is sometimes put at stake. Tight flight schedules or overwork of employees with insufficient pay may contribute to keeping the price of airplane tickets down, but they may also sometimes result in maintenance errors which may lead to fatal accidents.

　1つ目の要素については、サービスが良くないことをハイライト部分で述べ、具体的にどのような点でサービスが良くないのかについて、下線部で例を挙げています。誰もが共感あるいは想像ができるような、一般的な具体例です。自分が格安航空を利用して、不便な思いをしたのであれば、その経験について書いても良いかもしれません。ただし、自分の経験を書くと長くなりがちである点には注意すること。簡潔に、トピックからそれないように書きましょう。2つ目の要素については、ハイライト部分で安全性の懸念について触れ、続く下線部では、どうして安全性に欠けることがあるのか、その裏にある事情について説明して、文章中に大きな飛躍ができないようにしています。

このフレーズ、たいせつ！

- [ ] not all rainbows and butterflies
  良いことばかりではない
- [ ] put A at stake
  Aを危険にさらす
- [ ] tight flight schedule
  立て込んだスケジュール
- [ ] insufficient pay
  不十分な賃金
- [ ] fatal accident
  致命的な事故

Conclusion

14 Low-price airlines are becoming increasingly popular. Although these airlines do not provide the conveniences of more expensive airlines, they allow people to get to their destinations at lower costs. Discuss both the positive and negative aspects of low-price airlines and state your opinion.

訳 格安航空の人気が高まってきている。これらの航空会社は、より高額な航空会社ほどの利便性は提供しないが、格安で目的地にたどり着くことを可能にする。格安航空の良い面と悪い面の両方を論じ、自分の意見を述べなさい。

🔍 モデルエッセーより ||||||||||||||||||||||||||||||||||||||||||||||||||||||||||||||||||||||||||||||||||||||||||||||||||||||||||||||||||||||

Taking both the advantages and disadvantages of low-cost airlines into consideration, I stand by the opinion that these airlines can be beneficial as long as the prices are reasonably moderated so as not to impose an excessive burden on either the customers or employees.

訳 格安航空の長所と短所の両方を考慮した上で、私は、乗客と従業員のどちらにも過剰な負担を強いることがないよう値段が適切に調整されている限りは、これらの航空会社は有益であり得るという立場を取る。

解 説

要約文

▶ Taking both the advantages and disadvantages of low-cost airlines into consideration,

　文章全体をまとめるに当たり、長所と短所の両方を考慮したことをまず示しています。

結論文

▶ I stand by the opinion that these airlines can be beneficial as long as the prices are reasonably moderated so as not to impose an excessive burden on either the customers or employees.

　自分の意見を再度明示し、自分が格安航空を支持する条件を書いています。下線部では、「格安航空の料金が適切に調整されている限り」という条件つきで、「格安航空は有益であり得る」という結論を述べています。

このフレーズ、たいせつ！

☐ take A into consideration
Aについて考慮する

☐ impose an excessive burden on A
Aに対して過剰な負担を強いる

📖 交通に関連したコロケーション

☐ commute to work
通勤する

☐ use public transport
公共交通機関を利用する

☐ a delayed train
遅延した電車

☐ ignore the traffic light
信号を無視する

☐ reach the destination
目的地にたどり着く

☐ get a driving licence
運転免許を取得する

☐ take the underground
地下鉄を使う

☐ reduce traffic congestion
交通渋滞を減らす

☐ drive to a remote area
遠隔地に車で行く

☐ cross a pedestrian bridge
歩道橋を渡る

☐ limit the use of private vehicles
自家用車の利用を制限する

Task 2

15 社会がテーマの問題
Society [What Can We Do to Help the Poor?]

There are people who suffer from poverty in every country. What do you think the reasons for poverty are in your country and what do you think can be done to help these impoverished people?

Brainstorming

Introduction 指示文のパラフレーズと意見の提示をする

指示文のパラフレーズ：*although Japan is one of the most developed countries, a significant number of people live below the poverty line*

国が支援をすべき：*I think that society can provide various kinds of support to such people and their families to help end the negative spiral of poverty*

Body 1 1つ目の理由と解決策をまとめる

教育水準の低さ→経済的支援：*many people fall into poverty in Japan because they only have low levels of education → without a sufficient education, they cannot get a stable job and end up doing unstable jobs with low pay → in Japan, private schools often provide better education than public schools, going to a private school gives people better opportunities to achieve a good education → should provide financial support for low-income families to give their children better opportunities*

Body 2 2つ目の理由と解決策をまとめる

精神疾患→回復支援：*many people fall into poverty because they develop mental illnesses such as anxiety and depression → makes it hard for them to work stable jobs and they end up losing them → need to provide mental/clinical support at low costs to help these people recover and lift themselves out of poverty*

Body 3 3つ目の理由と解決策をまとめる

興味の対象が見つけにくい→仕事について知る機会の提供：*some people do not work because they have trouble discovering their interests and cannot find work that they can be truly passionate about → cannot find motivation → schools and universities should provide more opportunities for students to discover their interests*

Conclusion 上記を踏まえ全体をまとめる

まとめ：*should not provide just financial support for these people to get by → society (governments and education sector) should provide them with the means to lift themselves out of their impoverished state*

Model Essay

Introduction

Even in the global north, no one is guaranteed a life of wealth. Although Japan is one of the most developed countries in the world, a significant number of people live below the poverty line. In order to address this pressing social issue, it is imperative that the state provides adequate support to these people to help end the negative spiral of poverty.

Body 1

In Japan, many people fall into poverty because they only have a low level of education. Without sufficient education, it is difficult for them to get a stable job, so they end up doing unstable jobs with low pay. High-quality education in Japan is often extremely expensive and there are not many scholarships available. Therefore, more financial support systems should be created for low-income families to give their children better educational opportunities.

Body 2

Another major cause of poverty in Japan are mental illnesses such as anxiety and depression. Many people in Japan are overworked and feel excessive amounts of stress, which can trigger mental illness. Mental instability makes it hard for people to work stable full-time jobs. There is a need to provide mental support for free to help these people recover and lift themselves out of poverty.

Body 3

At the other end of the scale, some people do not work because they have trouble discovering their interests earlier on in their lives and cannot find work that they can be truly passionate about. In order to help young people discover their passions, schools and universities should provide more opportunities for students to learn about various jobs and think about their futures.

Conclusion

Concerning poverty in Japan, there are a number of factors which play into the current situation. In order to fix some of the problems, we need to provide various forms of social support to help people find their own way out of their unfavourable state.

(308 words)

Introduction

15 There are people who suffer from poverty in every country. What do you think the reasons for poverty are in your country and what do you think can be done to help these impoverished people?

訳 どの国にも貧困に苦しむ人々はいる。あなたの国における貧困の原因は何で、また、こうした貧困にある人々を助けるために何ができると思いますか？

🔍 モデルエッセーより ‖‖ ‖‖‖‖‖‖‖

Even in the global north, no one is guaranteed a life of wealth. Although Japan is one of the most developed countries in the world, a significant number of people live below the poverty line. In order to address this pressing social issue, it is imperative that the state provides adequate support to these people to help end the negative spiral of poverty.

訳 北の先進国といえども、誰もが豊かな生活を保障されているわけではない。日本は世界有数の先進国でありながら、かなりの数の人々が最低生活水準より下の暮らしをしている。この差し迫った社会的課題に対処するには、国がこれらの人々に適切な支援を提供し、貧困の負のスパイラルを止められるようにすることが不可欠である。

▷ 解 説

トピックについての一般的な事実

▶ Even in the global north, no one is guaranteed a
life of wealth. Although Japan is one of the most
developed countries in the world, a significant
number of people live below the poverty line.

　今回は、課題解決型のエッセーです。ここでは、誰も
がうなずける事実を述べます。読み手の注意を引くため
に、global north という示唆的な表現を用いています。こ
れは「主に北半球に偏在している先進国」を指します。

トピックのパラフレーズと自分の意見

▶ In order to address this pressing social issue, it is
imperative that the state provides adequate support
to these people to help end the negative spiral of
poverty.

　この文では、貧困の負のスパイラルに歯止めをかけるこ
との重要性を強調しています。この後の本論（Body）で
は、貧困の原因や解決法について述べていきます。

Body 1

15 There are people who suffer from poverty in every country. What do you think the reasons for poverty are in your country and what do you think can be done to help these impoverished people?

訳 どの国にも貧困に苦しむ人々はいる。あなたの国における貧困の原因は何で、また、こうした貧困にある人々を助けるために何ができると思いますか？

🔍 モデルエッセーより ||||||||||||||||||||||||||||||||||||||||||||||||||||||||||||||||||||||| |||||||||||

In Japan, many people fall into poverty because they only have a low level of education. Without sufficient education, it is difficult for them to get a stable job, so they end up doing unstable jobs with low pay. High-quality education in Japan is often extremely expensive and there are not many scholarships available. Therefore, more financial support systems should be created for low-income families to give their children better educational opportunities.

訳 日本においては、多くの人々が低い水準の教育しか受けていないために貧困に陥る。十分な教育を受けていないと、安定した仕事に就くことは困難で、最終的に不安定で賃金の低い仕事をすることになってしまう。日本では質の良い教育は非常に高価なことが多く、利用できる奨学金があまりない。そのため、低所得家庭の子どもたちにより良い教育の機会を与えるために、低所得家庭に対する経済的支援のシステムが作られるべきである。

---

 fall into の意味と使い方

fall into A は「急に A の状態に陥る」という意味の、ネガティブな状態を連想させるフレーズです。fall into poverty（貧困状態に陥る）や fall into a deep depression（深刻なうつ病状態に陥る）のように使います。また、「意図せずに始める」という意味もあり、fall into a bad habit（悪い癖がつく）という表現も頻出なので、まとめて覚えておきましょう。

解 説

主題文

▶ In Japan, many people fall into poverty because they only have a low level of education.

このエッセーは、自分の国での貧困の原因とその改善策について書く必要があるので、答え方も少し特殊になってきます。本論（Body）の構成としては、日本における貧困の原因をまず最初に挙げて、続いてその解決策を簡潔に述べる形式が良いでしょう。本論1（Body 1）では、貧困の1つ目の原因として「十分な教育が受けられないこと」を挙げています。

支持文

▶Without sufficient education, it is difficult for them to get a stable job, so they end up doing unstable jobs with low pay. High-quality education in Japan is often extremely expensive and there are not many scholarships available. Therefore, more financial support systems should be created for low-income families to give their children better educational opportunities.

下線部において、十分な教育を受けられないことが貧困につながる理由について説明しています。そして、ハイライト部分で解決策を述べています。モデルエッセーでは解決策はすべて非常に簡潔にしか書いていませんが、貧困の理由を2つに絞って、解決策の部分を多めに書くといった方法もあります。

この**単語**、たいせつ!

☐ scholarship
⊛奨学金

この**フレーズ**、たいせつ!

☐ get a stable job
安定した仕事に就く

Body 2

15 There are people who suffer from poverty in every country. What do you think the reasons for poverty are in your country and what do you think can be done to help these impoverished people?

訳 どの国にも貧困に苦しむ人々はいる。あなたの国における貧困の原因は何で、また、こうした貧困にある人々を助けるために何ができると思いますか？

モデルエッセーより ||||||||||||||||||||||||||||||||||||||||||||||||||||||||||||||||||||||| ||||||||||

Another major cause of poverty in Japan are mental illnesses such as anxiety and depression. Many people in Japan are overworked and feel excessive amounts of stress, which can trigger mental illness. Mental instability makes it hard for people to work stable full-time jobs. There is a need to provide mental support for free to help these people recover and lift themselves out of poverty.

訳 日本における貧困のもう1つの大きな要因は不安症やうつ病などの精神疾患である。日本の多くの人が、過重労働をしていて過剰なストレスを感じており、これが精神疾患の引き金となり得る。精神の不安定によって、常勤の定職で働くことが困難になる。このような人々が回復し、自ら貧困から抜け出せるようにするために、無償で精神的支援を提供する必要がある。

解説

主題文

▶ Another major cause of poverty in Japan are mental illnesses such as anxiety and depression.

　本論2（Body 2）では、貧困の2つ目の原因として「精神疾患」を挙げています。主題文において、不安障害やうつ病など具体例も挙げています。

支持文

▶ Many people in Japan are overworked and feel excessive amounts of stress, which can trigger mental illness. Mental instability makes it hard for people to work stable full-time jobs. There is a need to provide mental support for free to help these people recover and lift themselves out of poverty.

　下線部において、人々が精神疾患にかかる理由と、それが貧困につながる理由を説明しています。ハイライト部分では、簡単に解決策を示しています。

この**単語**、たいせつ！

- instability
  名 不安定さ

この**フレーズ**、たいせつ！

- anxiety and depression
  不安症やうつ病
- feel excessive amounts of stress
  過剰な量のストレスを感じる
- full-time job
  常勤の仕事

Body 3

15 There are people who suffer from poverty in every country. What do you think the reasons for poverty are in your country and what do you think can be done to help these impoverished people?

訳 どの国にも貧困に苦しむ人々はいる。あなたの国における貧困の原因は何で、また、こうした貧困にある人々を助けるために何ができると思いますか？

🔍 モデルエッセーより ||||||||||||||||||||||||||||||||||||||||||||||||||||||||||||||||||||||||||| |||||||||||

At the other end of the scale, some people do not work because they have trouble discovering their interests earlier on in their lives and cannot find work that they can be truly passionate about. In order to help young people discover their passions, schools and universities should provide more opportunities for students to learn about various jobs and think about their futures.

訳 その対極には、人生のより早い時期で自分の興味の対象をなかなか発見できず、心から情熱を注げる仕事を見つけることができないために、働かない人もいる。若者が夢中になれるものを発見できるように、学校や大学は学生がさまざまな仕事について知り、将来について考える機会をもっとたくさん提供すべきである。

 「困難」の表し方

「〜するのに困る」「〜することが大変である」という表現は、パラグラフの主題文でよく用いられます。have trouble -ing や have a hard time -ing よりも文語的な表現である have difficulty (in) -ing を、使えるようにしておきましょう。前置詞の with を用いた have difficulty with A（A に苦労する）も、一緒に覚えておきたい表現です。

解説

主題文

▶ At the other end of the scale, some people do not work because they have trouble discovering their interests earlier on in their lives and cannot find work that they can be truly passionate about.

　本論3（Body 3）では、貧困の3つ目の原因として働かない人がいるということを挙げ、その理由として「興味の対象を見いだせず、情熱を注げない」ということを、ハイライト部分で具体的に述べています。

支持文

▶ In order to help young people discover their passions, schools and universities should provide more opportunities for students to learn about various jobs and think about their futures.

　この文では、解決策を示しています。ハイライト部分で、「将来の仕事について考える機会を学校や大学が学生にもっとたくさん提供すべきである」と具体案を提示しています。

このフレーズ、たいせつ！

☐ be truly passionate about A
Aに心からの情熱がある

Conclusion

15 There are people who suffer from poverty in every country. What do you think the reasons for poverty are in your country and what do you think can be done to help these impoverished people?

訳 どの国にも貧困に苦しむ人々はいる。あなたの国における貧困の原因は何で、また、こうした貧困にある人々を助けるために何ができると思いますか？

モデルエッセーより ||||||||||||||||||||||||||||||||||||||||||||||||||||||||||||||||||||||||||||||||||| |||||||||||

Concerning poverty in Japan, there are a number of factors which play into the current situation. In order to fix some of the problems, we need to provide various forms of social support to help people find their own way out of their unfavourable state.

訳 日本の貧困問題に関しては、現在の状況を招く数多くの要因がある。このような問題のいくつかを解決するためには、さまざまな形の社会支援を提供し、人々が不利な状態から抜け出す方法を自ら見つけられるように支援する必要がある。

解 説

要約文

▶ Concerning poverty in Japan, there are a number of factors which play into the current situation.

要約文（Summarising Sentence）では、これまで述べてきたことに関し「数多くの要因がある」と簡潔にまとめています。ここでは具体例などの提示は避け、シンプルに書きましょう。

結論文

▶ In order to fix some of the problems, we need to provide various forms of social support to help people find their own way out of their unfavourable state.

結論文（Concluding Sentence）では解決法を提示し、主語をIではなくWeにすることで客観性を出しています。このような課題解決型のエッセーでは、結論で自分なりの解決法を述べるようにしましょう。

このフレーズ、たいせつ！

- [ ] social support
  社会的支援
- [ ] unfavourable state
  好ましくない状態

📖 国や社会に関連したコロケーション

- [ ] wealthy countries
  裕福な国
- [ ] developed countries
  先進国
- [ ] developing countries
  発展途上国
- [ ] emerging countries
  新興国
- [ ] pension system
  年金制度
- [ ] social welfare
  社会福祉
- [ ] gender stereotypes
  性に関する固定観念
- [ ] racial discrimination
  人種差別
- [ ] Western civilisation
  西洋文明
- [ ] equal opportunities
  機会均等

Task 2

16 犯罪がテーマの問題
Crime [Death Penalty: For or Against?]

The death penalty is the best form of punishment for people who commit serious crimes. To what extent do you agree or disagree with this statement?

Brainstorming

Introduction ▶ 指示文のパラフレーズと意見の提示をする

指示文のパラフレーズ：*in many countries, the death penalty is set as the principal form of punishment → those who commit serious crimes like murder are often sentenced to the death penalty*

死刑よりも無期懲役が有効：*I do not think that the death penalty is the most effective form of punishment for serious crime → life imprisonment is the best way to punish criminals*

Body 1 ▶ 1つ目の理由をまとめる

死刑になれば罪悪感を背負って生きなくてよくなる：*if they are put to death, criminals will not have to live with the guilt for what they did*
will not have time to think about their actions and the effect that it had on all of the people involved → I think that people who commit serious crimes should have to live their entire lives with the guilt → using the death penalty will only relieve them of this moral burden

Body 2 ▶ 2つ目の理由をまとめる

死刑を執行する人に精神的負担がかかる：*nobody actually wants to engage in the act of killing another human being → poses an emotional burden on those who have to carry out the death penalty → life imprisonment is less morally daunting for these people*
there are actually many cases where death penalties cannot be carried out because nobody wants to carry them out

Body 3 ▶ 3つ目の理由をまとめる

遺族にも、他人を死に追いやったという精神的負担がかかる：*even if families of victims want criminals to pay for their actions through the death penalty, it will still pose an emotional burden on them since they have to be conscious of the fact that they sent another human being to their death*

Conclusion ▶ 上記を踏まえ全体をまとめる

まとめ：*life imprisonment should be the highest penalty and not the death sentence → makes sure that criminals spend the rest of their lives paying for what they did and alleviates the stress and burden on other people*

Model Essay

Introduction

In many countries, those who commit serious crimes like murder are often sentenced to death as a way for them to pay for their actions. However, I do not think that the death penalty is the most effective form of punishment for serious crimes. I would suggest that life imprisonment be made the most severe sentence.

Body 1

Criminals should spend the rest of their lives carrying the guilt of what they did. If they are put to death, this means that there will be less time to contemplate their wrongdoings and to feel remorse towards all the people who were negatively affected by their criminal actions. Those who commit serious crimes should have to live their entire lives facing extreme shame and guilt. The death penalty will only relieve them of this lifelong moral burden.

Body 2

On top of this, nobody is actually willing to engage themselves in the act of killing another human being. Therefore, having to execute a criminal poses an emotional burden on those who actually have to carry out the sentence. There are many cases where death penalties cannot be carried out because nobody wants to do the dirty work. From this perspective, life imprisonment is less morally daunting for the authorities.

Body 3

Understandably, most families of victims want criminals to be sentenced to the most severe form of punishment. Even so, if the criminal is given the death penalty, it can still impose an emotional burden on these families since they will have to live with the pang of conscience for having sent another person to their death.

Conclusion

There are many reasons why people may theoretically favour the death penalty, but just as many convincing arguments why it does not work in practice. Life imprisonment should replace the death sentence as the highest penalty. It makes sure that criminals spend the rest of their lives paying for what they did and also alleviates the stress and burden on families and the authorities.

(324 words)

Introduction

16 The death penalty is the best form of punishment for people who commit serious crimes. To what extent do you agree or disagree with this statement?

訳 死刑は重大な罪を犯した人への最適な処罰の形である。あなたはこの意見にどの程度賛成あるいは反対しますか？

モデルエッセーより |||||||||||||||||||||||||||||||||||||||||||||||||||||||||||||||||||||||||||||||||||||||||||||||

In many countries, those who commit serious crimes like murder are often sentenced to death as a way for them to pay for their actions. However, I do not think that the death penalty is the most effective form of punishment for serious crimes. I would suggest that life imprisonment be made the most severe sentence.

訳 多くの国で、殺人などの重大な罪を犯した人は、しばしばその行為を償う方法として死刑を言い渡される。しかし、個人的には、死刑は重大犯罪に対する最も有効な処罰の形ではないと思う。私なら無期懲役が最も重い刑になるよう提案するだろう。

解 説

トピックについての一般的な事実

▶ In many countries, those who commit serious crimes like murder are often sentenced to death as a way for them to pay for their actions.

　ここでは、「多くの国で、重大な罪を犯した人は死刑に処される」という一般的な事実を述べています。those who を用いることで、人の特徴を後置修飾の形で表現しています。

トピックのパラフレーズと自分の意見

▶ However, I do not think that the death penalty is the most effective form of punishment for serious crimes. I would suggest that life imprisonment be made the most severe sentence.

　下線部で自分の意見を述べ、ハイライト部分では、無期懲役を最も重い刑にすることを提案しています。ただ死刑を否定するだけでは、「では、どうやって犯罪者に自分の罪を償わせたらいいのか」という疑問が読み手に残ってしまうので、このように代替案を提示することがポイントです。

この単語、たいせつ！

- [ ] murder
  - 名殺人
- [ ] sentence
  - 動判決を下す
- [ ] punishment
  - 名罰

このフレーズ、たいせつ！

- [ ] commit serious crimes
  - 重大な罪を犯す
- [ ] life imprisonment
  - 終身刑

Body 1

16 The death penalty is the best form of punishment for people who commit serious crimes. To what extent do you agree or disagree with this statement?

訳 死刑は重大な罪を犯した人への最適な処罰の形である。あなたはこの意見にどの程度賛成あるいは反対しますか？

モデルエッセーより ||||||||||||||||||||||||||||||||||||||||||||||||||||||||||||||||||||||||||||||||

Criminals should spend the rest of their lives carrying the guilt of what they did. If they are put to death, this means that there will be less time to contemplate their wrongdoings and to feel remorse towards all the people who were negatively affected by their criminal actions. Those who commit serious crimes should have to live their entire lives facing extreme shame and guilt. The death penalty will only relieve them of this lifelong moral burden.

訳 犯罪者は、自分がしたことへの罪悪感を抱えながら残りの人生を過ごすべきである。もし彼らが死刑になれば、自分の悪事について熟考し、その犯罪行為の悪影響を受けたすべての人々への自責の念に駆られる時間が短縮されることになる。重大な罪を犯した人は、究極の恥と罪悪感に向き合いながら全生涯を送るべきである。死刑は、この生涯続く倫理的な負担から彼らを解放するだけである。

▶ 解説

主題文

▶ Criminals should spend the rest of their lives carrying the guilt of what they did.

　このエッセーでは、本論1（Body 1）から本論3（Body 3）までの部分で1つずつ、死刑ではなく無期懲役を最高の刑罰とするべきだと考える理由を述べています。少しチャレンジングなのは、導入（Introduction）で「無期懲役を最高の刑罰にするべきである」という提案をしているので、各本論（Body）でも「なぜ死刑ではなく無期懲役なのか」について説明をある程度入れる必要があるという点です。この文では、1つ目の理由である「犯罪者は罪の意識を背負って残りの人生を送るべきである」ということについて書いています。

支持文

▶ If they are put to death, this means that there will be less time to contemplate their wrongdoings and to feel remorse towards all the people who were negatively affected by their criminal actions. Those who commit serious crimes should have to live their entire lives facing extreme shame and guilt. The death penalty will only relieve them of this lifelong moral burden.

　下線部で、死んでしまうと罪の意識も消えてしまうという視点から1つ目の理由を詳しく説明しています。そして、ハイライト部分で、「死刑にすると、倫理的な負担から解放されてしまう」ことについて述べ、無期懲役のほうがその点で有効であるということを示唆しています。

この単語、たいせつ！

- criminal
  (名) 犯罪者
- guilt
  (名) 罪悪感
- contemplate
  (動) 熟慮する
- wrongdoing
  (名) 悪事
- remorse
  (名) 自責
- relieve
  (動) 解放する

このフレーズ、たいせつ！

- death penalty
  死刑
- moral burden
  倫理的な負担

Body 2

16 The death penalty is the best form of punishment for people who commit serious crimes. To what extent do you agree or disagree with this statement?

訳 死刑は重大な罪を犯した人への最適な処罰の形である。あなたはこの意見にどの程度賛成あるいは反対しますか？

Q モデルエッセーより ||||||||||||||||||||||||||||||||||||||||||||||||||||||||||||||||||||||||||||||||||||||||| |||||||||||||

On top of this, nobody is actually willing to engage themselves in the act of killing another human being. Therefore, having to execute a criminal poses an emotional burden on those who actually have to carry out the sentence. There are many cases where death penalties cannot be carried out because nobody wants to do the dirty work. From this perspective, life imprisonment is less morally daunting for the authorities.

訳 これに加えて、実のところ、他の人間を殺す行為に関与したいという人は誰もいない。そのため、刑を実際に執行しなくてはならない人々に、犯罪者の処刑任務は精神的な負担を与える。誰も厄介な仕事をしたくないがゆえに、死刑が執行できないケースが多く存在する。この観点からすると、無期懲役のほうが（刑務関係の）職員の精神的な困難は少ない。

 追加のディスコースマーカー

also（また） ＊too や as well などよりも形式的
furthermore（さらに）
additionally（加えて）
in addition to A（A に加えて）
on top of A（A の上に、A に加えて） ＊通常、ネガティブな文脈で用いる

▶ 解 説

このフレーズ、たいせつ!

☐ on top of this
　その上
☐ execute a
　criminal
　犯罪者を処刑する
☐ emotional
　burden
　精神的な負担
☐ morally daunting
　道徳的に気が重い

主題文

▶ On top of this, nobody is actually willing to engage themselves in the act of killing another human being.

　この文では、2つ目の理由として「誰も死刑を執行したくはない」ということを述べています。「Aに加えて」を意味するディスコースマーカーの on top of A は、通常、ネガティブな事柄を追加する際の前置きに使います。

支持文

▶ Therefore, having to execute a criminal poses an emotional burden on those who actually have to carry out the sentence. There are many cases where death penalties cannot be carried out because nobody wants to do the dirty work. From this perspective, life imprisonment is less morally daunting for the authorities.

　下線部では、2つ目の理由を説明しています。また下線部の2文目では、死刑が実施されないケースが多く存在するという事実を述べることで、自分の意見を補強しています。実際に社会で起こっている問題やデータなどを用いるとかなり説得力が増しますね。そして、ハイライト部分で、無期懲役のほうがこの点に関しては有効であると述べています。

Body 3

16 The death penalty is the best form of punishment for people who commit serious crimes. To what extent do you agree or disagree with this statement?

訳 死刑は重大な罪を犯した人への最適な処罰の形である。あなたはこの意見にどの程度賛成あるいは反対しますか？

モデルエッセーより ||||||||||||||||||||||||||||||||||||||||||||||||||||||||||||||||||||||||

Understandably, most families of victims want criminals to be sentenced to the most severe form of punishment. Even so, if the criminal is given the death penalty, it can still impose an emotional burden on these families since they will have to live with the pang of conscience for having sent another person to their death.

訳 当然のことであるが、ほとんどの被害者遺族は犯罪者に最も重い処罰が下されることを求めている。そうだとしても、犯罪者が死刑になれば、他の人間を死に追いやったという良心の痛みを抱えて生きていかなければならないため、遺族には依然として精神的な負担がかかり得る。

▶ 解 説

主題文

▶ Understandably, most families of victims want criminals to be sentenced to the most severe form of punishment.

　本論1（Body 1）と本論2（Body 2）での主張に関する譲歩をするように、遺族側の意見を説明し理解を示しています。ディスコースマーカーでもあるUnderstandably を用いて、パラグラフ全体の内容を示唆しています。

支持文

▶ Even so, if the criminal is given the death penalty, it can still impose an emotional burden on these families since they will have to live with the pang of conscience for having sent another person to their death.

　Even so は前述の内容とは対照的な内容を展開するときに使う表現です。ハイライト部分のsince 以下で、遺族にとって精神的な負担になる理由を述べています。

この単語、たいせつ！

☐ victim
　图 被害者

このフレーズ、たいせつ！

☐ emotional burden
　精神的な負担
☐ pang of conscience
　良心の呵責

Conclusion

16 The death penalty is the best form of punishment for people who commit serious crimes. To what extent do you agree or disagree with this statement?

訳 死刑は重大な罪を犯した人への最適な処罰の形である。あなたはこの意見にどの程度賛成あるいは反対しますか？

Q モデルエッセーより ||||||||||||||||||||||||||||||||||||||||||||||||||||||||||||||||||

There are many reasons why people may theoretically favour the death penalty, but just as many convincing arguments why it does not work in practice. Life imprisonment should replace the death sentence as the highest penalty. It makes sure that criminals spend the rest of their lives paying for what they did and also alleviates the stress and burden on families and the authorities.

訳 人々が理論的に死刑を支持する理由はたくさんあるが、死刑が実際には機能しない理由を述べた説得力のある議論も、ちょうど同じくらいたくさんある。最高刑として、無期懲役が死刑に置き換えられるべきである。そうすれば、犯罪者が自分のしたことを償うために残りの人生を過ごすことが確実になり、また遺族や職員のストレスと負担を軽減することができる。

解 説

要約文

▶ There are many reasons why people may theoretically favour the death penalty, but just as many convincing arguments why it does not work in practice.

この文では本論（Body）の1～3のまとめを述べています。その際、本論で用いた表現の繰り返しは避け、別の表現にパラフレーズします。

結論文

▶ Life imprisonment should replace the death sentence as the highest penalty. It makes sure that criminals spend the rest of their lives paying for what they did and also alleviates the stress and burden on families and the authorities.

ここでは、助動詞shouldを用いて自分の主張を展開しています。賛成・反対型のエッセーでは、客観性を保ちながら自分の立ち位置を明確にしましょう。

この単語、たいせつ！

☐ theoretically
　副 理論的に
☐ favour
　動 より好む
☐ alleviate
　動 軽減する

このフレーズ、たいせつ！

☐ convincing argument
　説得力のある議論

📖 犯罪に関連したコロケーション

☐ high crime rate
　高い犯罪率
☐ arrest the criminal
　犯罪者を逮捕する
☐ investigate the crime scene
　犯罪現場を調査する
☐ justify a vile crime
　残酷な犯罪を正当化する
☐ detain the suspect
　容疑者を拘留する
☐ arrest the notorious robber
　その悪名高い泥棒を逮捕する
☐ witness a serial murder
　連続殺人を目撃する
☐ a guilty verdict
　有罪判決
☐ have a clear motive
　明確な動機がある
☐ socially unacceptable behaviour
　社会的に受け入れられない振る舞い

225

Task 2

17 ビジネスがテーマの問題

Business [Businesses Should Think of Profit as Their Highest Priority: For or Against?]

Businesses should put profit as their highest priority. To what extent do you agree or disagree with this opinion and are there any other aspects that you think companies should value?

☀ Brainstorming

Introduction ▶ 指示文のパラフレーズと意見の提示をする

指示文のパラフレーズ：*many companies prioritise making a large profit over anything else*

金銭的結果だけに集中すべきではない：*however, I think that just focusing on financial outcome makes companies forget about other important aspects*

Body 1 ▶ 1つ目の理由をまとめる

質の高いサービスと製品を提供すれば、信頼と名声が得られる：*companies should make sure that they provide quality services and products to consumers, even if it may cost more than providing mediocre or lower quality products*
→ *will gain customers' trust / more people will repeatedly buy their services or products*
→ *good reputation will bring even more customers*

Body 2 ▶ 2つ目の理由をまとめる

従業員を不幸にしないことが、損失を防ぐ：*companies often overwork their employees with insufficient pay*
→ *causes workers to become unhappy and tired*
→ *loss of employees' enthusiasm*
→ *major loss to the company*

Body 3 ▶ 3つ目の理由をまとめる

社会に良い影響を与えることが、好印象にもつながる：*should use some of their profit to have a positive impact on the whole of society or volunteer work*
→ *making better impression of company on society*

Conclusion ▶ 上記を踏まえ全体をまとめる

まとめ：*companies should not be fully focused on just making a profit*
→ *it will not be beneficial to the company in the long run*

Model Essay

Introduction

Many companies prioritise making a large profit over anything else. However, I personally think that just focusing on financial outcome makes companies forget about other important aspects. Such companies need to stop thinking in the here and now and reconsider their priorities from a more long-term perspective.

Body 1

One of the most essential things to a company is the trust of their customers. Companies should always make sure that they provide quality services and products to consumers, even if this may cost more than providing a huge supply of mediocre or lower quality products. Through always ensuring high quality of service and products, companies can create and maintain a good reputation. This reputation will attract more buyers and create a positive cycle which benefits both the business and its customers.

Body 2

Companies that only care about making money often overwork their employees with insufficient pay. This causes workers to become unhappy and tired, which results in lower work productivity. Since loss of employees' enthusiasm towards their job can be a major loss to the company, companies should always provide a safe and comfortable working environment for their employees.

Body 3

Lastly, companies should use some of their profit to have a positive impact on the whole of society. They should participate in or be the managers of charity projects or volunteer work. This not only helps to make the world a better place, but it also contributes to the company making a better impression on society.

Conclusion

For these reasons, companies should not be fully focused on just making a profit for it will not be beneficial to the company in the long run. Investment for the future is not just about immediate monetary gain, and developing the framework to make both customers and employees happy is likely to generate more sustainable success.   (298 words)

Introduction

17 Businesses should put profit as their highest priority. To what extent do you agree or disagree with this opinion and are there any other aspects that you think companies should value?

訳 企業は利益を得ることを最優先させるべきである。あなたはこの意見にどの程度賛成あるいは反対しますか？ また、他に企業が重視すべき側面はあると思いますか？

 モデルエッセーより |||||||||||||||||||||||||||||||||||||||||||||||||||||||||||||||||||||||||||||||||||||||| ||||||||||||

Many companies prioritise making a large profit over anything else. However, I personally think that just focusing on financial outcome makes companies forget about other important aspects. Such companies need to stop thinking in the here and now and reconsider their priorities from a more long-term perspective.

訳 多くの企業が、大きな利益を上げることを他の何よりも優先している。しかしながら、私は個人的に、金銭的な結果だけに集中すると、企業は他の大切な側面を忘れてしまうことになると考えている。そのような企業は、目先のことだけを考えるのをやめて、より長期的な観点から優先事項を見直す必要がある。

「観点」の表現

アカデミックライティングでは客観性が重要であるため、自分の意見を述べる際にも客観的・多角的な視点を示す必要があります。以下の表現を有効活用して、独り善がりでない説得力のある表現を心がけましょう。

from the perspective of A　（Aの観点から）
from a different perspective　（異なる観点から）
from a broader perspective　（より広い視野から）
from a historical point of view　（歴史的な観点から）
from a commercial perspective　（商業的な観点から）
from an educational perspective　（教育的な観点から）
from a business point of view　（ビジネスの観点から）
from a completely different perspective　（まったく違った観点から）
from a more short-term perspective　（より短期的な観点から）

▶ 解 説

トピックについての一般的な事実

▶ Many companies prioritise making a large profit over anything else.

　ここでは、多くの企業が他の何よりも利益を得ることを優先しているという一般的な事実を述べています。

トピックのパラフレーズと自分の意見

▶ However, I personally think that just focusing on financial outcome makes companies forget about other important aspects. Such companies need to stop thinking in the here and now and reconsider their priorities from a more long-term perspective.

　今回は自分の意見の部分を少し多めに書きました。下線部だけでも十分自分の意見を述べているのですが、ハイライト部分をつけ加えることで自分の意見を強調し、より印象づけています。

この単語、たいせつ!

☐ prioritise
　動 優先する
☐ profit
　名 利益
☐ reconsider
　動 再考する

このフレーズ、たいせつ!

☐ financial outcome
　金銭的な結果

Body 1

17 Businesses should put profit as their highest priority. To what extent do you agree or disagree with this opinion and are there any other aspects that you think companies should value?

訳 企業は利益を得ることを最優先させるべきである。あなたはこの意見にどの程度賛成あるいは反対しますか？ また、他に企業が重視すべき側面はあると思いますか？

 モデルエッセーより ||||||||||||||||||||||||||||||||||||||||||||||||||||||||||||||||||||| |||||||||||||

One of the most essential things to a company is the trust of their customers. Companies should always make sure that they provide quality service and products to consumers, even if this may cost more than providing a huge supply of mediocre or lower quality products. Through always ensuring high quality of service and products, companies can create and maintain a good reputation. This reputation will attract more buyers and create a positive cycle which benefits both the business and its customers.

訳 企業にとって最も肝心なことの1つは、顧客の信頼である。企業は、たとえそうすることで平凡もしくは品質の低い製品を大量に供給する場合よりもコストがかかろうと、常に、顧客に質の高いサービスと製品を確実に提供するべきである。質の高いサービスと製品を常に保証することで、企業は良い評判を生み、維持することができる。この評判がより多くの買い手を引きつけ、企業とその顧客の両方に利益のある好循環を作り出す。

重要さの表し方

important（重要な）
It is important to sign up this client.
（この顧客と契約を取ることは重要である）
critical（致命的で重要な）
This is a critical quarter for the banking industry.
（今回は銀行業界にとって重要な四半期である）
crucial（極めて決定的で重大な）
Thursday's budget will prove crucial for our future.
（木曜日の予算は、私たちの将来にとって極めて重要なものになるだろう）

vital（命に関わるほどの重要な）
The files contain vital information.
（ファイルには極めて重要な情報が含まれている）
significant（意義があり重要な）
There was a significant change in the company policy.
（会社の方針に大きな変更があった）
imperative（絶対的に必要な）
Hiring a competent replacement is imperative.
（有能な後任を雇うことが絶対的に必要である）

▶ 解 説

主題文

▶ One of the most essential things to a company is the trust of their customers.

　この文ではまず、企業にとって顧客の信頼が重要であることを述べています。

支持文

▶ Companies should always make sure that they provide quality service and products to consumers, even if this may cost more than providing a huge supply of mediocre or lower quality products. Through always ensuring high quality of service and products, companies can create and maintain a good reputation. This reputation will attract more buyers and create a positive cycle which benefits both the business and its customers.

　下線部では、質の高いサービスと製品を提供すべきであるという自分の意見を述べ、ハイライト部分でそれを裏づける具体的な理由を述べています。ビジネス関連のさまざまな語句を要所要所で使い、高得点につなげましょう。

この単語、たいせつ！

- [ ] essential
  - (形)重要な
- [ ] provide
  - (動)供給する
- [ ] mediocre
  - (形)平凡な
- [ ] ensure
  - (動)保証する
- [ ] reputation
  - (名)評判
- [ ] attract
  - (動)魅了する

このフレーズ、たいせつ！

- [ ] make sure
  - 確実にする
- [ ] create a positive cycle
  - 好循環を作る

Body 2

17 Businesses should put profit as their highest priority. To what extent do you agree or disagree with this opinion and are there any other aspects that you think companies should value?

訳 企業は利益を得ることを最優先させるべきである。あなたはこの意見にどの程度賛成あるいは反対しますか？ また、他に企業が重視すべき側面はあると思いますか？

 モデルエッセーより ||||||||||||||||||||||||||||||||||||||||||||||||||||||||||||||||| |||||||||||

Companies that only care about making money often overwork their employees with insufficient pay. This causes workers to become unhappy and tired, which results in lower work productivity. Since loss of employees' enthusiasm towards their job can be a major loss to the company, companies should always provide a safe and comfortable working environment for their employees.

訳 もうけることにしか関心のない企業は、しばしば不十分な給料で従業員を過度に働かせる。これにより、労働者は不幸かつ疲労した状態になり、労働生産性が低下する。従業員の仕事への熱意の喪失は会社にとって大きな損失になり得るため、企業は従業員に常に安全で快適な労働環境を提供するべきである。

！ さまざまな二項表現

二項表現（binomial expression）とは、convenient and beneficial（便利で有益な）などのように2つの単語を and でつないだ表現で、「類義語（synonyms）」「反意語（antonyms）」「押韻（rhyming）」「反復（repetition）」「頭韻（alliteration）」の5つに分類できます。

- **類義語（synonyms）**
  plain and simple（単純明白な）
  calm and quiet（穏やかで静かな）
- **反意語（antonyms）**
  black and white（白黒）
  bride and groom（新郎新婦）
- **押韻（rhyming）**
  meet and greet（面会して挨拶する）
  wine and dine（酒と料理）
- **反復（repetition）**
  over and over（何度も）
  again and again（再三再四）
- **頭韻（alliteration）**
  tried and tested（試行錯誤した）
  signed and sealed（署名捺印された）

解 説

主題文

▶ Companies that only care about making money often overwork their employees with insufficient pay. This causes workers to become <u>unhappy and tired</u>, which results in lower work productivity.

まず、十分な給料を支払わず利益を追求することが生産性の低下につながることを、簡潔にまとめています。下線部では、それの原因となる労働者の状態を二項表現で伝えています。

支持文

▶ Since loss of employees' enthusiasm towards their job can be a major loss to the company, companies should always provide a <u>safe and comfortable</u> working environment for their employees.

ここでは労働環境に関する解決策を提示しています。下線部のsafe and comfortable（安全で快適な）は、応用が利く頻出表現です。

この単語、たいせつ！

☐ overwork
⑩ 過度に働かせる

☐ enthusiasm
⑧ 熱意

このフレーズ、たいせつ！

☐ comfortable working environment
働きやすい仕事環境

Body 3

17 Businesses should put profit as their highest priority. To what extent do you agree or disagree with this opinion and are there any other aspects that you think companies should value?

訳 企業は利益を得ることを最優先させるべきである。あなたはこの意見にどの程度賛成あるいは反対しますか? また、他に企業が重視すべき側面はあると思いますか?

モデルエッセーより ||||||||||||||||||||||||||||||||||||||||||||||||||||||||||||||||||||||||||||||||||||||||||||||||||||

Lastly, companies should use some of their profit to have a positive impact on the whole of society. They should participate in or be the managers of charity projects or volunteer work. This not only helps to make the world a better place, but it also contributes to the company making a better impression on society.

訳 最後に、企業は、利益の一部を社会全体にプラスの影響を与えるために使うべきである。慈善事業やボランティア活動に参加したり、それを運営したりすべきである。これは世界をより良い場所にするのに役立つばかりでなく、その企業のより良い印象を社会に与えることにも貢献する。

解 説

主題文

▶ Lastly, companies should use some of their profit to have a positive impact on the whole of society.

このエッセーのように、本論（Body）を３つ使うこともあります。ディスコースマーカーのLastly（最後に）を用いて最後の意見であることを示し、会社の利益の使い方について主張しています。

支持文

▶ They should participate in or be the managers of charity projects or volunteer work. This not only helps to make the world a better place, but it also contributes to the company making a better impression on society.

ここでは慈善事業やボランティアなどの活動内容を具体的に示し、主題文での主張を強化しています。not only A but also Bの構文を用いることで、２つの要素を１文に簡潔にまとめることができます。

- [ ] participate
  動 参加する

この**フレーズ**、たいせつ！

- [ ] have a positive impact on A
  Aに良い影響を与える
- [ ] make a better impression on A
  Aにより良い印象を与える

Conclusion

17 Businesses should put profit as their highest priority. To what extent do you agree or disagree with this opinion and are there any other aspects that you think companies should value?

訳 企業は利益を得ることを最優先させるべきである。あなたはこの意見にどの程度賛成あるいは反対しますか？　また、他に企業が重視すべき側面はあると思いますか？

モデルエッセーより |||||||||||||||||||||||||||||||||||||||||||||||||||||||||||||||||||||||||||||||||||||

For these reasons, companies should not be fully focused on just making a profit for it will not be beneficial to the company in the long run. Investment for the future is not just about immediate monetary gain, and developing the framework to make both customers and employees happy is likely to generate more sustainable success.

訳 このような理由から、企業は利益を得ることだけに集中すべきではない。長い目で見てそれは企業にとって利益にならないからである。将来のための投資とは、単なる目先の金銭的利益のためのものではないし、顧客と従業員の双方が幸せになれるような仕組みを構築することで、より持続的な成功を生み出しやすくなるのである。

▶解 説

この単語、たいせつ!

☐ beneficial
形 有益な

要約文

▶ For these reasons, companies should not be fully focused on just making a profit for it will not be beneficial to the company in the long run.

本論の議論を要約した文です。下線部のFor these reasonsがディスコースマーカーの役目を果たし、助動詞のshouldが主張であることを示唆しています。

このフレーズ、たいせつ!

☐ in the long run
長い目で見て

結論文

▶ Investment for the future is not just about immediate monetary gain, and developing the framework to make both customers and employees happy is likely to generate more sustainable success.

締めくくりに、これまでに使った表現をimmediate monetary gain（目先の金銭的な利益）やgenerate more sustainable success（より持続的な成功を生み出す）といった高度な表現にパラフレーズしつつ、未来の展望を述べています。

📖 ビジネスに関連したコロケーション

☐ make a large profit
大きな利益を上げる

☐ ensure high quality
高い品質を保証する

☐ commodity prices
物価

☐ commercial products
商業商品

☐ market research
市場調査

☐ a business manoeuvre
経営戦略

☐ manipulate funds
資金を運用する

☐ start a new business
新しいビジネスを始める

☐ successful business
成功したビジネス

☐ profitable business
もうかるビジネス

18 法がテーマの問題

Law [Governments Should Control the Amount of Violence in Films and on TV: For or Against?]

Some state that governments should control the amount of violence on television in order to reduce the amount of violent crimes in society. However, others are against giving the government power to control the content of what people watch. Discuss both views and state your opinion on this matter.

Brainstorming

Introduction 指示文のパラフレーズと意見の提示をする

指示文のパラフレーズ：*violent scenes are often shown on easily accessible media such as TV*

For: governments should regulate the amount of violence shown on TV
→ *exposure to violence leads to high crime rates*
Against: governments should not control what people see on TV
政府にそこまでの権力を与えるべきではない：*I personally do not think that governments should be given so much power*

Body 1 賛成派の意見をまとめる

テレビで暴力を見ることが犯罪につながる→規制が必要：*seeing violence on TV can make serious crime increase*
→ *if people see fewer violent scenes, crime rates will go down*
→ *government regulations are the only power that can regulate the amount of violence on TV*
→ *would benefit society greatly*

Body 2 反対派の意見をまとめる

犯罪は暴力的シーン以外の要因でも起こる：*there is no clear coherence between serious crime commission and being exposed to violence in films and on TV*
→ *there must be other factors that make people commit crimes*
政府に頼らない規制も可能：*even if the government does not take legal measures, there are many other ways to prevent people from being overly exposed to violent scenes*
→ *encouraging parents to keep an eye on what their children watch*

Conclusion 上記を踏まえ全体をまとめる

まとめ：*I do not support the idea of governments placing strict regulations*
→ *it cannot be guaranteed that just doing this will reduce crime, and it could lead to the violation of people's freedom*

Model Essay

Introduction

Violent scenes are often shown on easily accessible media such as TV. Some people say that governments should regulate the amount of violence shown on TV since such exposure could lead people to become more inclined to commit serious crime. However, others are against strengthening governmental control. I personally do not think that governments should be given so much power as to control what people see on TV.

Body 1

Those who support the idea of governments controlling the amount of violence shown on TV are strong believers of the theory that seeing violence on TV makes serious crime rates increase. According to this particular view, if people see fewer violent scenes on TV, the number of serious crime cases will be reduced. Since it is difficult for private sectors to conduct extensive regulations, it would be best for governments to exercise their power to solve this issue.

Body 2

In contrast to this, there are a number of people who are more cautious about giving the government such unrestricted power. There must be other factors that make people commit crimes other than just seeing a few violent scenes on TV. For example, growing up in an unstable household, lack of sufficient education, and innate personality traits could also be triggers for crime. There should be milder ways to prevent people from being overly exposed to violence, such as introducing TV ratings, and encouraging parents to keep an eye on what their children watch.

Conclusion

Taking both viewpoints into full consideration, I do not support the idea of governments placing strict regulations on the amount of violence shown on TV. There is no guarantee that just doing this will actually reduce crime in society, and giving the government excessive power could lead to the violation of people's freedom.

(293 words)

Introduction

18 Some state that governments should control the amount of violence on television in order to reduce the amount of violent crimes in society. However, others are against giving the government power to control the content of what people watch. Discuss both views and state your opinion on this matter.

訳 社会における重大な犯罪を減らすために、テレビで放送される暴力（的なシーン）の量を政府が規制するべきだと主張する人もいる。しかし、その一方で、人々が（テレビで）見る内容を規制する権力を政府に与えることに反対する人もいる。両方の見解について論じ、この問題について自分の意見を述べなさい。

🔍 モデルエッセーより |||||||||||||||||||||||||||||||||||||||||||||||||||||||||||||||||||||||||||||||||| |||||||||||

Violent scenes are often shown on easily accessible media such as TV. Some people say that governments should regulate the amount of violence shown on TV since such exposure could lead people to become more inclined to commit serious crime. However, others are against strengthening governmental control. I personally do not think that governments should be given so much power as to control what people see on TV.

訳 暴力的なシーンは、テレビなどの簡単にアクセスできるメディアでよく放送されている。そのようなものにさらされることによって、重大な罪を犯す傾向が強まる人がいるかもしれないため、テレビで放送される暴力の量を政府が規制するべきであると言う人もいる。しかし、政府による規制の強化に反対する人もいる。個人的には、政府は人々がテレビで見る内容を規制するほどの権力を与えられるべきではないと考えている。

 短縮形は使わない

アカデミックライティングでは短縮形（contraction）を使いません。モデルエッセーでは I don't think ではなく I do not think と表現しています。他の語句も、例えば It's → It is、can't → cannot、won't → will not、There's → There is のように短縮せずに記述しましょう。

▶ 解 説

トピックについての一般的な事実

▶ Violent scenes are often shown on easily accessible media such as TV.

　暴力的なシーンがテレビでよく放送されるという、誰もがうなずける一般的な事実を述べています。always（いつも、必ず）などではなくoften（しばしば）を用い、ヘッジング（hedging）と呼ばれる控えめな表現にするのがポイントです。

トピックのパラフレーズと自分の意見

▶ Some people say that governments should regulate the amount of violence shown on TV since such exposure could lead people to become more inclined to commit serious crime. However, others are against strengthening governmental control. I personally do not think that governments should be given so much power as to control what people see on TV.

　指示文が長めなので、パラフレーズもその分少し長めになっています。そしてcontrolをより高度な表現であるregulateに言い換えています。逐語的にパラフレーズするのではなく、指示文から重要な要素を選択して言い換えるのがコツです。最後に下線部で、政府が権力を与えられるべきではないという意見を述べています。

Body 1

18 Some state that governments should control the amount of violence on television in order to reduce the amount of violent crimes in society. However, others are against giving the government power to control the content of what people watch. Discuss both views and state your opinion on this matter.

訳 社会における重大な犯罪を減らすために、テレビで放送される暴力（的なシーン）の量を政府が規制するべきだと主張する人もいる。しかし、その一方で、人々が（テレビで）見る内容を規制する権力を政府に与えることに反対する人もいる。両方の見解について論じ、この問題について自分の意見を述べなさい。

モデルエッセーより ||||||||||||||||||||||||||||||||||||||||||||||||||||||||||||||||||||||||| ||||||||||||

Those who support the idea of governments controlling the amount of violence shown on TV are strong believers of the theory that seeing violence on TV makes serious crime rates increase. According to this particular view, if people see fewer violent scenes on TV, the number of serious crime cases will be reduced. Since it is difficult for private sectors to conduct extensive regulations, it would be best for governments to exercise their power to solve this issue.

訳 テレビで放送される暴力の量を政府が規制することに賛成する人は、テレビで暴力を見ることで重大犯罪率が上がるという理論を強く支持している。この特定の見解によると、テレビで見る暴力的なシーンが減れば、重大犯罪の件数は減ることになる。私的機関が広範囲の規制を実施することは難しいため、政府が権力を行使してこの問題を解決するのが最善ということだろう。

研究などに言及する表現

According to this particular view（この特定の見解によると）
According to the research conducted by A（A によって行われた研究によると）
As shown in the recent research（最近の研究に見られるように）
It has been proven that ～（～ということが証明されている）
Studies have shown that ～（～ということが研究で分かっている）
Recent findings suggest that ～（最近の調査結果で～ということが分かっている）
Recent research clearly indicates that ～（最近の研究で明確になったことは～である）
Research has emerged that seems to contradict A.（A と矛盾するような研究結果も出てきている）
Research suggests this may not be the case.（そうではない可能性があることを示す研究結果がある）

解 説

主題文

▶ Those who support the idea of governments controlling the amount of violence shown on TV are strong believers of the theory that seeing violence on TV makes serious crime rates increase.

　ここでは、賛成派の意見をこれから書くということを示しています。賛成派の人たちはどうして賛成なのか、その裏にある事情について詳しく説明しています。

支持文

▶ According to this particular view, if people see fewer violent scenes on TV, the number of serious crime cases will be reduced. Since it is difficult for private sectors to conduct extensive regulations, it would be best for governments to exercise their power to solve this issue.

　下線部のように客観性が増す表現を積極的に用いましょう。ここでは、「テレビで放送される暴力が減れば重大犯罪の件数は減る」と「私的機関が大規模な規制を行うことは困難なため、政府が解決するのが最善」という2点を、賛成意見の根拠として挙げています。

この単語、たいせつ！

□ theory
　图 理論
□ reduce
　動 減らす

このフレーズ、たいせつ！

□ exercise one's power
　権力を行使する

Body 2

18 Some state that governments should control the amount of violence on television in order to reduce the amount of violent crimes in society. However, others are against giving the government power to control the content of what people watch. Discuss both views and state your opinion on this matter.

訳 社会における重大な犯罪を減らすために、テレビで放送される暴力（的なシーン）の量を政府が規制するべきだと主張する人もいる。しかし、その一方で、人々が（テレビで）見る内容を規制する権力を政府に与えることに反対する人もいる。両方の見解について論じ、この問題について自分の意見を述べなさい。

モデルエッセーより ||||||||||||||||||||||||||||||||||||||||||||||||||||||||||||||||||||||||||||||||||||||||||||

In contrast to this, there are a number of people who are more cautious about giving the government such unrestricted power. There must be other factors that make people commit crimes other than just seeing a few violent scenes on TV. For example, growing up in an unstable household, lack of sufficient education, and innate personality traits could also be triggers for crime. There should be milder ways to prevent people from being overly exposed to violence, such as introducing TV ratings, and encouraging parents to keep an eye on what their children watch.

訳 これとは対照的に、政府にそこまで際限のない権力を持たせてしまうことに慎重な人も多い。人々が罪を犯すことになる要因は、テレビで多少の暴力的なシーンを見ることよりも他にあるはずだ。例えば、不安定な家庭での生育や、十分な教育の欠如、生まれつきの性格的特徴なども、犯罪のきっかけになるかもしれない。テレビ（視聴制限）評価を導入する、子どもが何を見ているのか親が目を光らせるよう促すなど、人々がテレビを通して過度に暴力にさらされないようにするためのもっと穏やかな方法があるはずだ。

解説

主題文

▶ In contrast to this, there are a number of people who are more cautious about giving the government such unrestricted power.

　本論2（Body 2）では反対派の意見をまとめていきます。単に「反対派の人たちがいる」と表現するのではなく、表現を工夫しましょう。

支持文

▶ There must be other factors that make people commit crimes other than just seeing a few violent scenes on TV. For example, growing up in an unstable household, lack of sufficient education, and innate personality traits could also be triggers for crime. There should be milder ways to prevent people from being overly exposed to violence, such as introducing TV ratings, and encouraging parents to keep an eye on what their children watch.

　下線部が反対意見の理由であり、ハイライト部分においてそれぞれ、犯罪の他の要因と、より過激でない解決方法についての具体例を示しています。抽象的な内容の後に、しっかりと具体的な例を挙げることが重要です。

Conclusion

18 Some state that governments should control the amount of violence on television in order to reduce the amount of violent crimes in society. However, others are against giving the government power to control the content of what people watch. Discuss both views and state your opinion on this matter.

訳 社会における重大な犯罪を減らすために、テレビで放送される暴力（的なシーン）の量を政府が規制するべきだと主張する人もいる。しかし、その一方で、人々が（テレビで）見る内容を規制する権力を政府に与えることに反対する人もいる。両方の見解について論じ、この問題について自分の意見を述べなさい。

Q モデルエッセーより |||||||||||||||||||||||||||||||||||||||||||||||||||||||||||||||||||||||||||||||||||| |||||||||||

Taking both viewpoints into full consideration, I do not support the idea of governments placing strict regulations on the amount of violence shown on TV. There is no guarantee that just doing this will actually reduce crime in society, and giving the government excessive power could lead to the violation of people's freedom.

訳 両方の視点を十分に考慮した上で、私は、テレビで放送される暴力の量に政府が厳しい規制を設けるという案は支持しない。これ（政府による規制）を行うだけで社会における犯罪が減少するという保証はないし、政府に過剰な権力を与えることは、人々の自由の侵害にもつながり得るかもしれない。

解 説

要約文

▶ Taking both viewpoints into full consideration, I do not support the idea of governments placing strict regulations on the amount of violence shown on TV.

　自分の意見をここで再度はっきりと述べています。分詞構文を用いることで、文を簡潔にまとめています。

結論文

▶ There is no guarantee that just doing this will actually reduce crime in society, and giving the government excessive power could lead to the violation of people's freedom.

　政府が規制をしたからといって必ずしも犯罪が減るとは限らない上に、政府が大きな権力を持ち過ぎてしまうことは人々の自由の侵害にもつながり得る、というかなり発展的な内容を述べています。発展的な内容を書く際には、トピックからそれないように注意しましょう。

この単語、たいせつ!

☐ excessive
　㊡過剰な
☐ violation
　㊡侵害

このフレーズ、たいせつ!

☐ place strict regulations
　厳しい規制をかける

📖 **法律に関連したコロケーション**

☐ take legal action
　法的措置を取る
☐ government sponsorship
　政府出資
☐ prohibit smoking
　喫煙を禁じる
☐ prevent discrimination
　差別を防ぐ
☐ maintain a social norm
　社会的規範を維持する

☐ criticise the government
　政府を批判する
☐ govern the country
　国を統治する
☐ reach a consensus
　同意に至る
☐ negotiate with the government
　政府と交渉する
☐ introduce a new restriction
　新しい規則を導入する

Task 2

19 教育がテーマの問題

Education [Learning Foreign Languages at School: For or Against?]

Some people think that there is no need to require students to learn a foreign language at school. Do you think that students should be required to learn a foreign language at school? Why or why not?

Brainstorming

Introduction 指示文のパラフレーズと意見の提示をする

不要だという声もあるが、生徒には外国語学習を義務づけるべき：

though some people say that it is unnecessary, students should be required to learn foreign languages as part of their school education

Body 1 1つ目の理由をまとめる

外国語を知ることで、人とのコミュニケーションや知識、機会が広がる：

knowing a different language will help them to communicate with more people in the future → helps them to access more information and broaden their opportunities

Body 2 2つ目の理由をまとめる

他の国や文化を学ぶことで、広い視野や客観性が得られる：

students can learn about other countries and cultures → helps them to broaden their perspective and nurture flexible understanding towards the cultures and values of people from other countries → helps them to view their own country through an objective lens

Conclusion 上記を踏まえ全体をまとめる

まとめ：*students should be required to learn a foreign language → it will help them to gain the skills that they need to live and work in a globalising world*

Model Essay

Introduction

In today's society, languages play a pivotal role in global communications. Though some people say that it is unnecessary, students should be required to learn foreign languages as part of their school education. I believe that learning other languages has the following two benefits for students.

Body 1

Knowing a different language will help students to communicate with more people in the future. Even if they are not perfectly fluent in the language that they learn, having a certain amount of knowledge in another language will help them to interact and make connections with people who speak that language. Students will be able to learn more about the world and create new opportunities for themselves through such encounters with people from other countries.

Body 2

Moreover, when students learn another language, they learn more than just the language itself. Through studying another language, students are also introduced to the history, society, and culture of the country in which the target language is spoken. This will help them to broaden their perspective and nurture a flexible understanding towards the cultures and values of people from other countries. Gaining an insight into another country will also allow students to view their own country through an objective lens. Knowing about one's own country and also having a high tolerance for diversity will benefit students in the future when they have to work in a rapidly globalising world.

Conclusion

Students should definitely be required to learn a foreign language at school since it will help them to gain valuable skills that they need to live and work in today's ever-globalising world. Knowing another language can open up a whole new world for young students.

(275 words)

Introduction

19 Some people think that there is no need to require students to learn a foreign language at school. Do you think that students should be required to learn a foreign language at school? Why or why not?

訳 学校で生徒に外国語を学ぶことを義務づける必要はないと主張する人もいる。学校で生徒は外国語学習を義務づけられるべきだと思いますか？そう思う理由は何ですか？

モデルエッセーより ||||||||||||||||||||||||||||||||||||||||||||||||||||||||||||||||||||||||||||||||||

In today's society, languages play a pivotal role in global communications. Though some people say that it is unnecessary, students should be required to learn foreign languages as part of their school education. I believe that learning other languages has the following two benefits for students.

訳 現代社会で、言語はグローバルなコミュニケーションにおける極めて重要な役割を担っている。不要であると言う人もいるが、学校教育の一環として、生徒に外国語の学習を義務づけるべきである。私は、外国語を学ぶことは、生徒にとって次の2つの利点があると考えている。

💬 一般文で使える表現

アカデミックライティングの導入（Introduction）における一般文（General Statement）では、誰もがうなずける事実や最近の傾向について述べます。一般文で使える「型」を身につけ、スムーズに書き始められるようにしましょう。

in today's society（今日の社会では）
in this globalised society（このグローバル化する社会で）
in a rapidly globalising world（急速にグローバル化する世界で）
in today's ever-globalising world（今日のグローバル化し続ける世界で）
in this increasingly interconnected society（このますます密接につながる社会で）
There has been a controversy over A.（A を巡っては論争が行われてきた）
There has been an increasing concern about A.（A に対する懸念が高まっている）
The past two decades saw a rapid growth of A.（この 20 年間で A は急成長を遂げた）
Recent years have witnessed an increasing number of A.（近年、A の数が増えている）
In recent years, very little attention has been paid to A.
（近年、A についてはほとんど注目されていない）

解 説

トピックについての一般的な事実

▶ In today's society, languages play a pivotal role in global communications. Though some people say that it is unnecessary, students should be required to learn foreign languages as part of their school education.

　導入（Introduction）では、誰もがうなずける一般文（General Statement）で読み手を引きつけた後、外国語学習の義務化については賛否があることを述べています。

トピックのパラフレーズと自分の意見

▶ I believe that learning other languages has the following two benefits for students.

　エッセー全体の主題文（Thesis Statement）では、これから2つの利点を述べることを下線部で示唆し、自分の立ち位置を明確にしています。ここでは詳細は述べず、この後の本論（Body）で具体的な理由や根拠を示します。

Body 1

19 Some people think that there is no need to require students to learn a foreign language at school. Do you think that students should be required to learn a foreign language at school? Why or why not?

訳 学校で生徒に外国語を学ぶことを義務づける必要はないと主張する人もいる。学校で生徒は外国語学習を義務づけられるべきだと思いますか？そう思う理由は何ですか？

モデルエッセーより

Knowing a different language will help students to communicate with more people in the future. Even if they are not perfectly fluent in the language that they learn, having a certain amount of knowledge in another language will help them to interact and make connections with people who speak that language. Students will be able to learn more about the world and create new opportunities for themselves through such encounters with people from other countries.

訳 異なる言語を知ることは、生徒が将来より多くの人とコミュニケーションを取ることを可能にする。学んだ言語を完全に流暢に話せなくても、外国語について一定量の知識を持っていることは、その言語を話す人と触れ合い、つながる手助けとなる。外国人とのこうした出会いを通して、生徒は、世界についてより多くのことを知り、自ら新たな機会を作り出せるようになる。

解説

主題文

▶ Knowing a different language will help students to communicate with more people in the future.

　本論1（Body 1）では、「外国語を学ぶと生徒がより多くの人とコミュニケーションを取ることができるようになる」という利点を挙げています。

支持文

▶ Even if they are not perfectly fluent in the language that they learn, having a certain amount of knowledge in another language will help them to interact and make connections with people who speak that language. Students will be able to learn more about the world and create new opportunities for themselves through such encounters with people from other countries.

　ここでは、主題文での主張を補強する「理由」を述べています。下線部では、より多くの人とコミュニケーションを取れるとどのような利益があるのかについて説明しています。

このフレーズ、たいせつ！

☐ fluent in the language
その言語が流暢である

☐ create new opportunities
新しい機会を作る

Body 2

19 Some people think that there is no need to require students to learn a foreign language at school. Do you think that students should be required to learn a foreign language at school? Why or why not?

訳 学校で生徒に外国語を学ぶことを義務づける必要はないと主張する人もいる。学校で生徒は外国語学習を義務づけられるべきだと思いますか？そう思う理由は何ですか？

🔍 モデルエッセーより ||||||||||||||||||||||||||||||||||||||||||||||||||||||||||||||||||| |||||||||||

Moreover, when students learn another language, they learn more than just the language itself. Through studying another language, students are also introduced to the history, society, and culture of the country in which the target language is spoken. This will help them to broaden their perspective and nurture a flexible understanding towards the cultures and values of people from other countries. Gaining an insight into another country will also allow students to view their own country through an objective lens. Knowing about one's own country and also having a high tolerance for diversity will benefit students in the future when they have to work in a rapidly globalising world.

訳 さらに、生徒が他の言語を学ぶとき、彼らは単なる言語そのもの以上のことを学ぶのである。他の言語を勉強することを通して、生徒は対象言語が話されている国の歴史、社会、文化の手ほどきも受ける。このことは、彼らが視野を広げ、外国人の文化や価値観に対する柔軟な理解を養うことにつながる。また、他の国への見識を深めることによって、生徒は自分の国を客観的に見ることができるようになる。自分の国についての知識があり、多様性への高度な寛容さも持っていることは、将来、急速にグローバル化していく世界で働くことになった際に、生徒にとって有利になるだろう。

解説

主題文

▶ Moreover, when students learn another language, they learn more than just the language itself. Through studying another language, students are also introduced to the history, society, and culture of the country in which the target language is spoken.

　ここでは、2つ目の利点として、生徒は言語を学ぶ際に、その言語そのものについてだけ学ぶわけではなく、他にも学べることがあるという内容を下線部で記しています。他に学べるものは何なのかについては、ハイライト部分で述べられています。

支持文

▶ This will help them to broaden their perspective and nurture a flexible understanding towards the cultures and values of people from other countries. Gaining an insight into another country will also allow students to view their own country through an objective lens. Knowing about one's own country and also having a high tolerance for diversity will benefit students in the future when they have to work in a rapidly globalising world.

　下線部2カ所で、その言語が話されている国の歴史、社会、文化について知ることが生徒にとって有益である理由を示しています。そして最後の文で、そのことが、急速にグローバル化していく世界で将来、生徒たちが働くことになった際に有利に作用するだろうと、長期的な視点から論じています。

この単語、たいせつ！

☐ tolerance
　⑧寛容さ

このフレーズ、たいせつ！

☐ target language
　目標言語

☐ nurture flexible understanding
　柔軟性のある理解をはぐくむ

☐ through an objective lens
　客観的な視点を通して

☐ in a rapidly globalising world
　急速にグローバル化する世界で

Conclusion

19 Some people think that there is no need to require students to learn a foreign language at school. Do you think that students should be required to learn a foreign language at school? Why or why not?

訳 学校で生徒に外国語を学ぶことを義務づける必要はないと主張する人もいる。学校で生徒は外国語学習を義務づけられるべきだと思いますか？そう思う理由は何ですか？

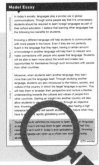

モデルエッセーより

Students should definitely be required to learn a foreign language at school since it will help them to gain valuable skills that they need to live and work in today's ever-globalising world. Knowing another language can open up a whole new world for young students.

訳 今日のグローバル化し続ける社会で生活し働くために必要な、価値あるスキルを身につけるのに役立つので、生徒は外国語を学校で学ぶことを間違いなく義務づけられるべきである。他の言語についての知識があれば、若い学生にとってまったく新しい世界が切り開かれるのである。

解 説

要約文

▶ Students should definitely be required to learn a foreign language at school since it will help them to gain valuable skills that they need to live and work in today's ever-globalising world.

結論として、today's ever-globalising world（今日のグローバル化し続ける社会）という描写を含め、ここまでに挙げた 2 つの理由と自分の主張をまとめています。

結論文

▶ Knowing another language can open up a whole new world for young students.

「他の言語を知っていることで新しい世界を切り開ける」という展望で締めくくります。結論は、このように未来の展望で締めくくることがよくあります。

このフレーズ、たいせつ！

- [ ] gain valuable skills
  価値のあるスキルを身につける
- [ ] open up a whole new world
  まったく新しい世界を切り開く

教育に関連したコロケーション

- [ ] fluent in the language
  その言語が流暢である
- [ ] meaningful interaction
  意味のあるやりとり
- [ ] become an autonomous learner
  自立した学習者になる
- [ ] quit a prestigious university
  一流大学を辞める
- [ ] intellectual growth
  知性の発達
- [ ] acquire transferrable skills
  移行可能なスキルを習得する
- [ ] compulsory subjects
  必須科目
- [ ] major in psychology
  心理学を専攻する
- [ ] learning opportunities
  学習の機会
- [ ] educational institution
  教育機関

Task 2

20 家族がテーマの問題
Family [How Can Families Be Brought Closer Together?]

Nowadays, families do not have close relationships like they once had. Explain what you think the reasons are for this and state your opinion on how this problem can be solved.

⟍Brainstorming

Introduction ▶ 指示文のパラフレーズと意見の提示をする

指示文のパラフレーズ：*family members used to have lifelong close relationships* ➜ *however, modern lifestyles are making families not as close as they used to be*
かつては近くにいて関係も密だった：*used to live together or close by* ➜ *assisted each other in daily life*
意識的な努力で解決できる：*with a little conscious effort, they can be resolved*

Body 1 ▶ 1つ目の理由と解決策をまとめる

個人主義の重視→自分のための時間と家族のための時間のバランスを取る：
people value individualism more than before ➜ *they still love and cherish their families, but they also value pursuing their own individual dreams and careers, even if pursuing them will involve spending less time with or even moving away from their families* ➜ *need to find a healthy balance between the time we make for ourselves and the time we set aside for our families*

Body 2 ▶ 2つ目の理由と解決策をまとめる

現代の技術でつながりを保てる→対面でのやりとりの大切さを認識する：
people can stay emotionally connected with their families with modern technology ➜ *can video call them cheaply, text them, mail them* ➜ *we need to acknowledge that meeting them in person is the best form of interaction and that we need to put in the time, money, and effort to meet them and spend time with them in person* ➜ *need to realise that digital interactions cannot fully make up for in-person interactions*

Conclusion ▶ 上記を踏まえ全体をまとめる

まとめ：*families are becoming less connected with each other due to modern changes in society and our personal lifestyles/values* ➜ *we cannot reverse these modern changes, so we need to learn to value connections with our families and make the time and effort to stay connected with them*

258

Model Essay

Introduction

Family members used to have lifelong close relationships, mainly because they lived together or close by and therefore had more daily communication with each other. However, modern families are not as close as they used to be. I think that there are two main reasons for this, and that with a little conscious effort, this contemporary issue can be resolved.

Body 1

In many countries, people now emphasise individualism and value pursuing their own goals and dreams. This does not necessarily mean that we no longer love our families. It just shows that there has been a shift in the balance of what we consider important in our lives. Unfortunately, chasing our dreams often involves investing more of our time in study or work, leaving less time for family. There is a need for us to be conscious about finding a healthy balance between the time we make for ourselves and the time we set aside for our families.

Body 2

Another reason why family bonds are not as tight as before is that people often feel somewhat connected with their families through modern technology. As ironic as it may be, knowing that we can easily call or text our loved ones anytime makes us subconsciously lazy about actually reaching out to them. We need to be aware that just feeling connected is not enough and that we must make the effort to actually communicate with our families, preferably in person.

Conclusion

Families are becoming less connected with each other due to modern changes in lifestyle. It is impossible to reverse these modern changes, so we need to learn to consciously make the time and effort to stay connected with our loved ones.

(278 words)

Introduction

20 Nowadays, families do not have close relationships like they once had. Explain what you think the reasons are for this and state your opinion on how this problem can be solved.

訳 昨今、家族はかつてのような強いつながりを持っていない。このことの理由をどう考えるか説明し、この問題をどう解決できるかについて自分の意見を述べなさい。

🔍 モデルエッセーより ||||||||||||||||||||||||||||||||||||||||||||||||||||||||||||||||||||| |||||||||||

Family members used to have lifelong close relationships, mainly because they lived together or close by and therefore had more daily communication with each other. However, modern families are not as close as they used to be. I think that there are two main reasons for this, and that with a little conscious effort, this contemporary issue can be resolved.

訳 かつて家族には、生涯にわたる強いつながりがあった。それは主に、一緒に住んでいたり、近くに住んでいたりしたため、日常の相互コミュニケーションを今より取れていたからである。しかし、現代の家族はかつてほど親密でない。これには主に2つの理由があり、少しの意識的な努力によって、この現代的な課題を克服できると私は考える。

▶ 解 説

トピックについての一般的な事実

▶Family members used to have lifelong close relationships, mainly because they lived together or close by and therefore had more daily communication with each other.

今回の問題は、課題解決型のエッセーで、あるテーマについて賛成・反対という意見を述べるものとは大きく異なります。この問題では、家族のつながりがかつてほど強くなくなってしまった理由とそれに対する解決策を述べる必要があります。モデルエッセーでは、本論1（Body 1）と本論2（Body 2）においてそれぞれ理由とそれに対する解決策を1つずつ述べる形になっています。

トピックのパラフレーズと自分の意見

▶However, modern families are not as close as they used to be. I think that there are <u>two main reasons</u> for this, and that with a little conscious effort, this contemporary issue can be <u>resolved</u>.

家族のつながりが弱くなってしまった理由をいくつ述べるのかを明記し、どのようにそれを解決していくのか、理由と解決策の両方について述べるということを、下線部で示唆しています。指示文の内容を十分に理解していることの表れになります。

このフレーズ、たいせつ！

☐ close relationship
親密な関係

☐ conscious effort
意識的な努力

☐ contemporary issue
現代的な課題

Body 1

20 Nowadays, families do not have close relationships like they once had. Explain what you think the reasons are for this and state your opinion on how this problem can be solved.

訳 昨今、家族はかつてのような強いつながりを持っていない。このことの理由をどう考えるか説明し、この問題をどう解決できるかについて自分の意見を述べなさい。

モデルエッセーより ||||||||||||||||||||||||||||||||||||||||||||||||||||||||||||||||||||||||||| |||||||||||

In many countries, people now emphasise individualism and value pursuing their own goals and dreams. This does not necessarily mean that we no longer love our families. It just shows that there has been a shift in the balance of what we consider important in our lives. Unfortunately, chasing our dreams often involves investing more of our time in study or work, leaving less time for family. There is a need for us to be conscious about finding a healthy balance between the time we make for ourselves and the time we set aside for our families.

訳 多くの国で今、人々は個人主義を重要視しており、自分の目標や夢を追い求めることに価値を置いている。これは必ずしも、私たちがもう家族を愛していないということではない。このことが示しているのは、単に、私たちが人生において重要と見なすもののバランスに変化が生じているということなのだ。残念なことに、自分の夢を追い求めると、多くの場合、より多くの時間を勉強や仕事に費やすことになり、これによって家族のための時間が少なくなってしまう。私たちは、自分のために作る時間と家族のために取っておく時間との間で、健全なバランスを意識的に保つ必要がある。

▶ 解 説

この単語、たいせつ！

☐ individualism
 (名)個人主義
☐ pursue
 (動)追求する
☐ chase
 (動)追いかける
☐ invest
 (動)投資する

このフレーズ、たいせつ！

☐ set aside
 取っておく

主題文

▶ In many countries, people now emphasise individualism and value pursuing their own goals and dreams.

　本論1 (Body 1) では家族のつながりが弱くなっている1つ目の理由とその解決策を述べています。この文では、現代の人たちは個人主義に基づき、自分自身の目標や夢を追うことを重視しているという理由を挙げています。

支持文

▶ This does not necessarily mean that we no longer love our families. It just shows that there has been a shift in the balance of what we consider important in our lives. Unfortunately, chasing our dreams often involves investing more of our time in study or work, leaving less time for family. There is a need for us to be conscious about finding a healthy balance between the time we make for ourselves and the time we set aside for our families.

　読み手にとってより共感しやすく、かつ極端な解釈をされない内容にするために、下線部で、個人主義が台頭したからといって家族を軽視するようになったわけではない、という補足をしています。自分が伝えたいことを相手に誤解されないように、明確に記すことが必要です。ハイライト部分では解決策を提示しています。

Body 2

20 Nowadays, families do not have close relationships like they once had. Explain what you think the reasons are for this and state your opinion on how this problem can be solved.

訳 昨今、家族はかつてのような強いつながりを持っていない。このことの理由をどう考えるか説明し、この問題をどう解決できるかについて自分の意見を述べなさい。

モデルエッセーより ||||||||||||||||||||||||||||||||||||||||||||||||||||||||||||||||||||||||||||||||| ||||||||||||

Another reason why family bonds are not as tight as before is that people often feel somewhat connected with their families through modern technology. As ironic as it may be, knowing that we can easily call or text our loved ones anytime makes us subconsciously lazy about actually reaching out to them. We need to be aware that just feeling connected is not enough and that we must make the effort to actually communicate with our families, preferably in person.

訳 家族の絆が以前ほど強固でないもう1つの理由は、人々がしばしば、現代の技術を通してなんとなく家族とつながっているように感じていることである。皮肉なことかもしれないが、いつでも簡単に大切な人に電話をかけたり、メッセージを送ったりできると分かっているため、実際に連絡を取ることに対して無意識のうちに怠惰になるのである。つながっているように感じるだけでは不十分であり、できれば対面で、実際に家族とコミュニケーションを取るために努力しなければならないということを、私たちは認識する必要がある。

解 説

主題文

▶ Another reason why family bonds are not as tight as before is that people often feel somewhat connected with their families through modern technology.

本論2（Body 2）ではもう1つの理由とその解決策について述べることになります。下線部の表現を入れることによって、ここからはもう1つ別の理由について書くということを明確にしています。

支持文

▶ As ironic as it may be, knowing that we can easily call or text our loved ones anytime makes us subconsciously lazy about actually reaching out to them. We need to be aware that just feeling connected is not enough and that we must make the effort to actually communicate with our families, preferably in person.

一般的にはスマートフォンやパソコンなどの現代技術によって人々のコミュニケーションが増えたと言われていますが、ここではあえてそれのマイナスの側面について書いています。いつでも連絡できると思うからこそ、連絡する回数が少なくなってしまうということを説明するに当たり、それが皮肉なことかもしれないと前置きしています。そして、ハイライト部分で解決策を簡潔に述べています。このように一般的に言われていることから離れた意見を書く際には、詳細な説明をする必要があります。

この**単語**、たいせつ！

- [ ] ironic
  - 形 皮肉な
- [ ] subconsciously
  - 副 無意識に
- [ ] preferably
  - 副 できれば

この**フレーズ**、たいせつ！

- [ ] family bonds
  - 家族の絆

Conclusion

20 Nowadays, families do not have close relationships like they once had. Explain what you think the reasons are for this and state your opinion on how this problem can be solved.

訳 昨今、家族はかつてのような強いつながりを持っていない。このことの理由をどう考えるか説明し、この問題をどう解決できるかについて自分の意見を述べなさい。

 モデルエッセーより ||||||||||||||||||||||||||||||||||||||||||||||||||||||||||||||||||||||||||||||||||||||||||||||||||||

Families are becoming less connected with each other due to modern changes in lifestyle. It is impossible to reverse these modern changes, so we need to learn to consciously make the time and effort to stay connected with our loved ones.

訳 現代における生活様式の変化によって、家族同士のつながりは希薄になりつつある。こうした現代的な変化を逆戻りさせることは不可能なので、私たちは大切な人とつながりを保つために意識的に時間を作り、努力をするすべを身につける必要がある。

▶ 解 説

要約文

▶ Families are becoming less connected with each other due to <u>modern changes in lifestyle</u>.

2つの異なる理由をどのようにまとめるかは難しいところです。ここでは下線部のように、現代の生活様式の変化としてまとめています。

結論文

▶ It is impossible to reverse these modern changes, <u>so we need to learn to consciously make the time and effort to stay connected with our loved ones</u>.

下線部で家族との時間を意識的に作り出し、努力しなければならないことを強調して結論を導いています。課題解決型のエッセーでは、最後に何かしらの解決策や提案をして締めくくりましょう。

この単語、たいせつ！

□ reverse
　⑩逆にする

このフレーズ、たいせつ！

□ stay connected with A
　Aとつながり続ける

📖 家族に関連したコロケーション

□ modern family
　現代の家族

□ nuclear family
　核家族

□ family structure
　家族構成

□ raise a child
　子どもを育てる

□ bond between family members
　家族間での絆

□ responsible parents
　責任のある親

□ overprotective parents
　過保護な親

□ spoiled child
　甘やかされた子ども

□ sibling rivalry
　兄弟間の競争

□ celebrate a wedding anniversary
　結婚記念日を祝う

Memo

おわりに

　ここまでのライティングの旅、いかがでしたでしょうか？ 本書の厳選した20問と洗練された英文に触れた方には、IELTSのライティング高得点のための「型」が見えてきたはずです。そして、多彩な表現への言い換えである「パラフレーズ」の重要性も認識できたのではないでしょうか。

　本書のエッセンスを学び取った後は、これまでインプットしてきたことを応用し、さらに磨きをかける形で、アウトプットを繰り返してください。どのようなコンテクストでも活用できるオリジナルの「型」が確立されれば、IELTSのあらゆるテーマに対応できます。そして、アカデミックライティングの「型」は、IELTSの次の世界でも役立ちます。また、ここで身につけた語彙や表現を活用して、シンプルな表現をアカデミックで高度な表現に「パラフレーズ」する習慣をつけていきましょう。

　今後は、日常で目にする英文を批判的に分析しながら、自分ならどう表現するかイメージするのも良いでしょう。アウトプットを意識することで、遭遇した表現を自分のコンテクストに置き換え、自分事として捉え、使える形で身につけることができます。

　英字新聞や英語の放送も、IELTSのライティングに使える洗練された表現の宝庫です。皆さんのこれからのさらなる旅を応援しています！

嶋津幸樹

世界へ羽ばたく
準備を
IELTS で

◆英文作成協力

Govindi Deerasinghe（ゴヴィンディ・ディラシンハ）

1994年スリランカ生まれ。9歳のときにイギリスに移住。ロンドン大学（UCL）卒業後、法律大学にて法廷弁護士資格取得。ロンドン大学大学院クイーンメアリー校にて、国際公法修士課程修了。IELTS 9.0満点取得。現在は、タクトピア株式会社のELT（英語教育）コンサルタントとして執筆活動を行う傍ら、人権問題を扱うNGOに所属している。

◆編集協力

髙橋彩夏（たかはし・あやか）

1995年茨城県生まれ。5歳から10歳までの間をアメリカのフロリダ州で過ごし、現地校で学ぶ。慶應義塾大学文学部人文社会学科教育学専攻卒。英検1級、TOEFL 118点、IELTS 8.5取得。シンガポールの高校で英語教員としての勤務経験を持つ。現在はシンガポールの企業に勤務する傍ら、ロンドン大学大学院（University of London）に在籍。

タクトピアIELTS研究チーム

庄司康介（東京外国語大学国際社会学部卒）

横井裕子（ニューヨーク州立大学卒）

中山依美（国際基督教大学卒）

辻村隆文（一橋大学社会学部卒）

安田彩夏（法政大学グローバル教養学部卒）

伊藤弥季南（早稲田大学文学部卒）

Asia Dobbs（ハワイ大学大学院卒）

塩野博之（グリネル大学卒）

河西真理（サンクトペテルブルク大学大学院卒）

児玉紅葉（カリフォルニア大学ロサンゼルス校卒）

菅谷菜々香（国際基督教大学大学院在籍）

日下美季（カリフォルニア大学アーバイン校在籍）

上野啓太（ミネルバ大学在籍）

山根愛里（マギル大学在籍）

タクトピアメンバー

渡邉慎也（コロンビア大学大学院卒）

早﨑綾（バーミンガム大学大学院卒）

田中大幸（ケント大学大学院卒）

北嶋友香（デポー大学卒）

◆著者プロフィール

嶋津幸樹 (しまづ・こうき)

1989年山梨県生まれ。17歳のときに海外進学塾を創業。青山学院大学文学部英米文学科卒。ロンドン大学教育研究所応用言語学修士課程修了。ケンブリッジ大学認定英語教授資格CELTA取得、IELTS 8.0取得。Pearson ELT Teacher Award 2017受賞。現在はタクトピア株式会社にてELT（英語教育）ディレクターを務める傍ら、大学講師やIELTS講師として活動中。著書に『改訂新装版 IELTSスピーキング完全対策』（アルク）などがある。

改訂新装版
IELTSライティング完全対策

※本書は、2022年に株式会社DHCより刊行された『IELTSライティング完全対策 第2版』を増補・改訂したものです。

発行日：2024年2月22日（初版）

著者：嶋津幸樹

協力：Govindi Deerasinghe、髙橋彩夏、タクトピアIELTS研究チーム
編集：株式会社アルク 文教編集部
校正：渡邉真理子、Peter Branscombe、Margaret Stalker
カバーデザイン：山之口正和（OKIKATA）
本文デザイン：株式会社Sun Fuerza
イラスト：いけがみますみ
カバー写真：菅原幹人
DTP・印刷・製本：株式会社Sun Fuerza

発行者：天野智之
発行所：株式会社アルク
〒102-0073 東京都千代田区九段北4-2-6 市ヶ谷ビル
Website：https://www.alc.co.jp/

地球人ネットワークを創る

アルクのシンボル
「地球人マーク」です。